Independent Task Force Report No. 80

Confronting Reality in Cyberspace

Foreign Policy for a Fragmented Internet

Nathaniel Fick and Jami Miscik, *Chairs*
Adam Segal, *Project Director*
Gordon M. Goldstein, *Deputy Project Director*

The Council on Foreign Relations (CFR) is an independent, nonpartisan membership organization, think tank, and publisher dedicated to being a resource for its members, government officials, business executives, journalists, educators and students, civic and religious leaders, and other interested citizens in order to help them better understand the world and the foreign policy choices facing the United States and other countries. Founded in 1921, CFR carries out its mission by maintaining a diverse membership, with special programs to promote interest and develop expertise in the next generation of foreign policy leaders; convening meetings at its headquarters in New York and in Washington, DC, and other cities where senior government officials, members of Congress, global leaders, and prominent thinkers come together with Council members to discuss and debate major international issues; supporting a Studies Program that fosters independent research, enabling CFR scholars to produce articles, reports, and books and hold roundtables that analyze foreign policy issues and make concrete policy recommendations; publishing *Foreign Affairs*, the preeminent journal on international affairs and U.S. foreign policy; sponsoring Independent Task Forces that produce reports with both findings and policy prescriptions on the most important foreign policy topics; and providing up-to-date information and analysis about world events and American foreign policy on its website, CFR.org.

The Council on Foreign Relations takes no institutional positions on policy issues and has no affiliation with the U.S. government. All views expressed in its publications and on its website are the sole responsibility of the author or authors.

The Council on Foreign Relations sponsors Independent Task Forces to assess issues of current and critical importance to U.S. foreign policy and provide policymakers with concrete judgments and recommendations. Diverse in backgrounds and perspectives, Task Force members aim to reach a meaningful consensus on policy through private deliberations. Once launched, Task Forces are independent of CFR and solely responsible for the content of their reports. Task Force members are asked to join a consensus signifying that they endorse "the general policy thrust and judgments reached by the group, though not necessarily every finding and recommendation." Each Task Force member also has the option of putting forward an additional or a dissenting view. Members' affiliations are listed for identification purposes only and do not imply institutional endorsement. Task Force observers participate in discussions, but are not asked to join the consensus.

For further information about CFR or this Task Force, please write to the Council on Foreign Relations, 58 East 68th Street, New York, NY 10065, or call the Communications office at 212.434.9888. Visit our website, CFR.org.

This report is printed on paper that is FSC® Chain-of-Custody Certified by a printer who is certified by BM TRADA North America Inc.

TASK FORCE MEMBERS

Task Force members are asked to join a consensus signifying that they endorse "the general policy thrust and judgments reached by the group, though not necessarily every finding and recommendation." They participate in the Task Force in their individual, not institutional, capacities.

Nicholas F. Beim
Venrock

Elizabeth Bodine-Baron
RAND Corporation

Guillermo S. Christensen★
*Association of U.S.
Cyber Forces (AUSCF)*

Michael Dempsey
Northrop Grumman

Nathaniel Fick
Elastic

Gordon M. Goldstein
Council on Foreign Relations

Vishaal Hariprasad
Resilience

Niloofar Razi Howe
Energy Impact Partners

Will Hurd
Former Member of Congress

Richard H. Ledgett Jr.
Hakluyt & Company

Shelley B. Leibowitz
SL Advisory, LLC

Eric H. Loeb
Salesforce

Kimberly Marten
*Barnard College,
Columbia University*

Evan S. Medeiros
Georgetown University

Jami Miscik
Kissinger Associates, Inc.

Joseph S. Nye Jr.★
Harvard Kennedy School

Nicole Perlroth
Cybersecurity Author and Advisor

Neal A. Pollard★
Ernst & Young

Samantha F. Ravich
*Foundation for Defense
of Democracies*

Ted Schlein
Kleiner Perkins

Adam Segal
Council on Foreign Relations

Camille A. Stewart
Google LLC

Philip J. Venables
Google LLC

Zaid A. Zaid
Cloudflare, Inc.

Amy B. Zegart★
Stanford University

*The individual has endorsed the report and signed an additional view.

iii

CONTENTS

FOREWORD

The internet is a vital part of modern life, providing a backbone for critical civilian infrastructure, facilitating global digital trade, and promoting the exchange of ideas. When most of this country (and the world) went into a months-long lockdown due to the COVID-19 pandemic, the internet allowed us to continue conducting business, preventing a total economic meltdown.

The United States has heavily influenced every step of the internet's development. The technologies that undergird the internet were born out of U.S. federal research projects, while U.S. companies and technical experts made significant contributions. Similarly, the internet's governance structures reflected American values, with a reliance on the private sector and technical community, light regulatory oversight, and the protection of speech and the promotion of the free flow of information.

For many years, this global internet served U.S. interests, and U.S. leaders often called for countries to embrace an open internet or risk being left behind. But this utopian vision became just that: a vision, not the reality. Instead, over time the internet became less free, more fragmented, and less secure. Authoritarian regimes have managed to limit its use by those who might weaken their hold and have learned how to use it to further repress would-be or actual opponents.

The lack of regulation around something so integral to modern economies, societies, political systems, and militaries has also become dangerous. This openness presents a tempting target for both states and nonstate actors seeking to undermine democracy, promote terrorism, steal intellectual property, and cause extraordinary disruption. Even more dangerous is the vulnerability of critical infrastructure to cyberattacks. Making the circumstances all the more difficult, figuring out who is behind a given attack remains challenging, allowing states and nonstate actors to carry out cyberattacks with a high degree of deniability and avoid significant consequences. In addition, because most cyberattacks occur well below the threshold of the use of force, the threat of retaliation is less credible.

Frankly, U.S. policy toward cyberspace and the internet has failed to keep up. The United States desperately needs a new foreign policy that confronts head on the consequences of a fragmented and dangerous internet.

This Task Force has done much to analyze the present dangers and the failure of policymakers to stop or reverse the trend toward further fragmentation. The Task Force concludes that—among other things—the era of the global internet is over; Washington will be unable to stop further fragmentation; data is a source of geopolitical competition, the United States has taken itself out of the digital trade sphere (undercutting Washington's ability to lead abroad); cybercrime is a pressing national security threat; and Washington and its allies have failed to impose sufficient consequences on attackers.

To confront the realities of the modern internet and adapt to today's cyber realm, the Task Force recommends an approach resting on three pillars. The first calls for the United States to bring together a coalition of allies and partners around a vision of the internet that preserves a trusted, protected international communication platform. The second pillar calls for the United States to employ more targeted diplomatic and economic pressure on adversaries that choose to attack critical infrastructure. Finally, as is a trend across almost all walks of U.S. policy these days, the United States should put its own proverbial house in order, blending digital competition policy with national security strategy. The Task Force concludes that the United States cannot afford to wait to reconsider its cyber policy and must instead act urgently to confront the new realities of cyberspace and develop strategies to ameliorate the pressing threat that exists.

This report provides a realistic look at cybersecurity and foreign policy, one informed by analytical candor and practical recommendations. It deserves a wide and careful reading. I would like to thank the Task Force chairs, CFR Board Members Nathaniel Fick and Jami Miscik, for their leadership and significant contributions to this project. My gratitude extends to all the Task Force members and observers for lending their knowledge and expertise, especially when their time is in such high demand. I also thank CFR's Adam Segal, who directed the Task Force and authored this report, Gordon M. Goldstein, who served as deputy director, Robert Knake, who initially launched the project before returning to government service, and Anya Schmemann, who guided the entire project as Task Force program director. They have all earned our gratitude for taking on this important subject.

Richard Haass
President
Council on Foreign Relations
July 2022

ACKNOWLEDGMENTS

The report of the Independent Task Force on Cybersecurity is the product of its members and observers, who dedicated their time and expertise to developing a thoughtful U.S. foreign policy rooted in the reality of modern cyberspace. It was a pleasure to work with such an impressive group of individuals.

Task Force Co-chairs Nate Fick and Jami Miscik, in particular, deserve our deepest thanks for their energizing leadership and innovative thinking at every stage of this project. We hope the report reflects their sharp insights and guidance; we know they were a pleasure to work with, and for that we are grateful.

We are also indebted to former CFR Fellow Rob Knake, who served as this Task Force's initial project director before he returned to government service. Rob set a strong foundation for us, and his deep knowledge and creative ideas are evident in the final product.

Though all Task Force members and observers were generous with their input, we would like to give special thanks to Michael Dempsey, Niloo Razi Howe, Eric Loeb, Joe Nye, Neal Pollard, and Amy Zegart for providing extensive feedback and suggestions. The report also benefited from consultation with several external experts. We thank Dmitri Alperovitch, Kevin Mandia, and General Paul Nakasone for speaking to the Task Force and Jen Easterly and Chris Inglis for meeting with our leadership team. Although we gained advice from many people, we are responsible for the final content of the report, and any omissions or errors are our own.

Our gratitude extends to our CFR colleagues, without whom this report would not exist. We especially want to recognize Anya Schmemann, director of the Independent Task Force Program, for expertly managing this project from its inception and her teammates

Chelie Setzer and Connor Sutherland, whose daily efforts supporting the Task Force's work were indispensable. Research Associate Kyle Fendorf diligently assisted us with research and note-taking. We thank colleagues on the Publications team, the Product and Design team, and several interns, all of whom are listed at the end of this report. We are also grateful to our colleagues across CFR who have facilitated the report's distribution and outreach efforts, ensuring its messages reach their intended audience.

Finally, our thanks go to CFR President Richard Haass for supporting our efforts and allowing us the opportunity to direct this important project.

Adam Segal
Project Director

Gordon M. Goldstein
Deputy Project Director

INDEPENDENT
TASK FORCE REPORT

EXECUTIVE SUMMARY

The global internet—a vast matrix of telecommunications, fiber optics, and satellite networks—is in large part a creation of the United States. The technologies that underpin the internet grew out of federal research projects, and U.S. companies innovated, commercialized, and globalized the technology. The internet's basic structure—a reliance on the private sector and the technical community, relatively light regulatory oversight, and the protection of speech and the promotion of the free flow of information—reflected American values.

Moreover, U.S. strategic, economic, political, and foreign policy interests were served by the global, open internet. Washington long believed that its vision of the internet would ultimately prevail and that other countries would be forced to adjust to or miss out on the benefits of a global and open internet.

The United States now confronts a starkly different reality. The utopian vision of an open, reliable, and secure global network has not been achieved and is unlikely ever to be realized. Today, the internet is less free, more fragmented, and less secure.

Countries around the world now exert a greater degree of control over the internet, localizing data, blocking and moderating content, and launching political influence campaigns. Nation-states conduct massive cyber campaigns, and the number of disruptive attacks is growing. Adversaries are making it more difficult for the United States to operate in cyberspace. Parts of the internet are dark marketplaces for vandalism, crime, theft, and extortion.

Malicious actors have exploited social media platforms, spread disinformation and misinformation, incited disparate forms of political participation that can sway elections, engendered fierce violence, and promoted toxic forms of civic division.

At the same time, the modern internet remains a backbone for critical civilian infrastructure around the world. It is the main artery of global digital trade. It has broken barriers for sharing information, supports grassroots organization and marginalized communities, and can still act as a means of dissent under repressive government regimes.

As the Internet of Things (IoT) expands in coming years, the next iteration of the network will connect tens of billions of devices, digitally binding every aspect of day-to-day life, from heart monitors and refrigerators to traffic lights and agricultural methane emissions.

The United States, however, cannot capture the gains of future innovation by continuing to pursue failed policies based on an unrealistic and dated vision of the internet.

The United States needs a new strategy that responds to what is now a fragmented and dangerous internet. The Task Force believes it is time for a new foreign policy for cyberspace.

The major findings of the Task Force are as follows:

- The era of the global internet is over.

- U.S. policies promoting an open, global internet have failed, and Washington will be unable to stop or reverse the trend toward fragmentation.

- Data is a source of geopolitical power and competition and is seen as central to economic and national security.

- The United States has taken itself out of the game on digital trade, and the continued failure to adopt comprehensive privacy and data protection rules at home undercuts Washington's ability to lead abroad.

- Increased digitization increases vulnerability, given that nearly every aspect of business and statecraft is exposed to disruption, theft, or manipulation.

- Most cyberattacks that violate sovereignty remain below the threshold for the use of force or armed attack. These breaches are generally used for espionage, political advantage, and international statecraft, with the most damaging attacks undermining trust and confidence in social, political, and economic institutions.

- Cybercrime is a national security risk, and ransomware attacks on hospitals, schools, businesses, and local governments should be seen as such.

- The United States can no longer treat cyber and information operations as two separate domains.

- Artificial intelligence (AI) and other new technologies will increase strategic instability.

- The United States has failed to impose sufficient costs on attackers.

- Norms are more useful in binding friends together than in constraining adversaries.

- Indictments and sanctions have been ineffective in stopping state-backed hackers.

The Task Force proposes three pillars to a foreign policy that should guide Washington's adaptation to today's more complex, variegated, and dangerous cyber realm.

First, Washington should confront reality and consolidate a coalition of allies and friends around a vision of the internet that preserves—to the greatest degree possible—a trusted, protected international communication platform.

Second, the United States should balance more targeted diplomatic and economic pressure on adversaries, as well as more disruptive cyber operations, with clear statements about self-imposed restraint on specific types of targets agreed to among U.S. allies.

Third, the United States needs to put its own proverbial house in order. That requirement calls for Washington to link more cohesively

COUNCIL on FOREIGN RELATIONS

58 East 68th Street, New York, New York 10065
tel 212.434.9400 fax 212.434.9800 www.cfr.org

Dear Colleague:

As co-chairs of the bipartisan CFR-sponsored Independent Task Force on Cybersecurity, we are pleased to share with you a copy of the group's consensus report, *Confronting Reality in Cyberspace: Foreign Policy for a Fragmented Internet.*

The early advantages the United States and its allies held in cyberspace have largely disappeared as the internet has become increasingly fragmented, more dangerous, and less free. China and Russia in particular are working to export their authoritarian models of the internet around the world. While freedom on the internet declines, threats in cyberspace grow. Cybercrime and cyberattacks on critical infrastructure have cost billions of dollars worldwide and disrupted thousands of lives.

And while the U.S. response has focused on domestic policy and resilience, more attention should be paid to rethinking a vision of foreign policy for cyberspace. The report outlines a strategy founded on three pillars: building a trusted internet coalition, employing more targeted pressure on adversaries and establishing pragmatic cyber norms, and getting the U.S. house in order.

We hope you will find it of interest.

Sincerely,

Nathaniel Fick and Jami Miscik
Task Force Chairs

its policy for digital competition with the broader enterprise of national security strategy.

The major recommendations of the Task Force are as follows:

- Build a digital trade agreement among trusted partners.

- Agree to and adopt a shared policy on digital privacy that is interoperable with Europe's General Data Protection Regulation (GDPR).

- Resolve outstanding issues on U.S.-European Union (EU) data transfers.

- Create an international cybercrime center.

- Launch a focused program for cyber aid and infrastructure development.

- Work jointly across partners to retain technology superiority.

- Declare norms against destructive attacks on election and financial systems.

- Negotiate with adversaries to establish limits on cyber operations directed at nuclear command, control, and communications (NC3) systems.

- Develop coalition-wide practices for the Vulnerabilities Equities Process (VEP).

- Adopt greater transparency about defend forward actions.

- Hold states accountable for malicious activity emanating from their territories.

- Make digital competition a pillar of the national security strategy.

- Clean up U.S. cyberspace by offering incentives for internet service providers (ISPs) and cloud providers to reduce malicious activity within their infrastructure.

- Address the domestic intelligence gap.

- Promote the exchange of and collaboration among talent from trusted partners.

- Develop the expertise for cyber foreign policy.

A free, global, and open internet was a worthy aspiration that helped guide U.S. policymakers for the internet's first thirty years. The internet as it exists today, however, demands a reconsideration of U.S. cyber and foreign policies to confront these new realities. The Task Force believes that U.S. goals moving forward will be more limited and thus more attainable, but the United States needs to act quickly to design strategies and tactics that can ameliorate an urgent threat.

INTRODUCTION

The era of the global internet is over. Washington has worked closely over the last three decades with the private sector and allies to promote a vision of a global, open, secure, and interoperable internet, but the reality of cyberspace is now starkly different. The internet is more fragmented, less free, and more dangerous. Moreover, U.S. policymakers have long assumed that the global, open internet served American strategic, economic, political, and foreign policy interests. They believed that authoritarian, closed systems would struggle to hold back the challenges, both domestic and international, that a global network would present. This has not proved to be the case.

The early advantages the United States and its allies held in cyberspace have largely disappeared. The United States is asymmetrically vulnerable because of high levels of digitization and strong protections for free speech. Adversaries have adapted more rapidly than anticipated. They have a clear vision of their goals in cyberspace, developing and implementing strategies in pursuit of their interests, and have made it more difficult for the United States to operate unchallenged in this domain.

Around the world, states of every regime type are forcing the localization of data, as well as blocking and moderating content. The United States' early lead in internet technologies motivated many countries to promote data residency and other regulations to protect national companies. China has long blocked access to foreign websites, created trade barriers to U.S. technology companies, and given preference to domestic incumbents, which now operate across the globe. European policymakers are increasingly focused on the need for presumptive digital self-sufficiency and data privacy. Beijing and Moscow, in particular, have used the United Nations and other international organizations to promulgate a vision of cyber sovereignty centered on state control over the internet.

The international competition for power is accelerating the fragmentation of technology spheres. Policymakers in the United States and China worry about intelligence agencies introducing backdoors in software and hardware, interdicting products along the supply chain, and using both legal and extralegal means to access data held by technology firms. As a result, both countries have recently introduced new rules and measures designed to secure supply chains, exclude foreign suppliers and products, and control the flow of data.

The war between Russia and Ukraine has furthered the fracturing, with Moscow throttling American social media, including banning Facebook, Instagram, and Twitter. Apple, Cisco, Microsoft, Oracle, and others ended sales to or shut down services in Russia. Two American ISPs, Cogent and Lumen, disconnected from Russian networks.[1]

Internet freedom, as defined by qualitative and quantitative analyses, has been in decline for more than a decade (see figure 1). The advocacy group Freedom House, which tracks internet freedom across the world, has seen sustained declines in empirical measures of internet freedom, especially in Asia and the Middle East.[2] More states are launching political influence campaigns, hacking the accounts of activists and dissidents, and sometimes targeting vulnerable minority populations. A growing number of states choose to disconnect entirely from the global internet. According to the digital human rights group Access Now, at least 182 internet shutdowns across 34 countries occurred in 2021, compared with 196 cases across 25 countries in 2018.[3]

Threats in cyberspace continue to grow in both number and severity. Security has never been a feature of the internet; indeed, its original design prioritized openness and interoperability over security. Only recently have concepts such as *zero trust*—a framework requiring all users to be authenticated, authorized, and continuously validated for security—become widely accepted and practiced. Competitiveness in cyberspace will therefore be determined by the ability to operate effectively in an inherently insecure and compromised environment.

The majority of state-backed cyber operations remain related to espionage, but cyberattacks are also weapons of sabotage and disinformation, and the number of disruptive attacks is growing (see figure 2). Russia-based hackers are alleged to be responsible for attacks on the power grid in Kyiv in 2015 and 2016, and the Russian-sponsored 2017 NotPetya attack wiped data from the computers of banks, power

Figure 1. INTERNET FREEDOM HAS DECLINED IN RECENT YEARS

Changes in countries' internet freedom scores from 2014 to 2021

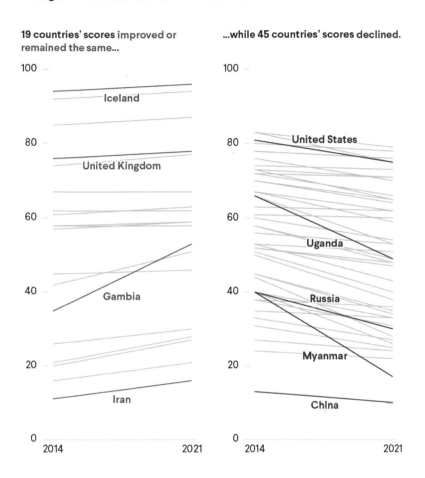

19 countries' scores improved or remained the same...

...while 45 countries' scores declined.

Notes: A higher score indicates higher internet freedom. The score is an index by Freedom House with ratings for indicators such as obstacles to internet access, limits on content, and violations of user rights. All countries with data for both 2014 and 2021 are included.

To view an interactive version of this chart, visit www.cfr.org/Cyberspace.

Source: Freedom House.

companies, gas stations, and government agencies, reportedly costing companies more than $10 billion worldwide.[4]

In the weeks before the Russian invasion of Ukraine, malware that can erase hard drives was found in Ukrainian government networks; hackers conducted spear-phishing campaigns against Ukraine's defense partners; threat actors pre-positioned themselves in supply chains for future attacks on Ukraine and the North Atlantic Treaty Organization (NATO); and distributed denial of service attacks briefly rendered the websites of banks and government organizations inaccessible. Russian hackers disrupted ViaSat, a provider of broadband satellite internet services, in the early hours of the invasion, and the effects spread from Ukraine to Germany and other parts of Europe. In early April, Ukrainian defenders prevented a destructive attack on Ukraine's power grid.[5] According to research from Microsoft, six groups linked to the Russian government conducted hundreds of operations designed to degrade Ukrainian institutions and disrupt access to information and critical services. In some instances, Russia's cyberattacks were "strongly correlated and sometimes directly timed with its kinetic military operations."[6]

Cybercrime on its own has become a threat to national security. Attacks on hospitals, schools, and local governments have disrupted thousands of lives. The Conti ransomware group shut down the administrative body in Ireland charged with managing the national health-care system, disrupting critical health treatments. A ransomware attack on Colonial Pipeline by a criminal group known as Darkside resulted in the shutdown of a 5,500-mile pipeline and gas shortages on the U.S. eastern seaboard. Another group, REvil, was reportedly the sponsor of an attack on U.S. meat supplier JBS that disrupted one-fifth of the nation's meat supply. This sharp rise in the volume and cost of ransomware incidents has had a dramatic effect on the cyber insurance markets, driving premiums up in excess of 100 percent.[7]

The digital battlefield is a complex space, and nonstate actors play a powerful role in cyber conflict: some state actors moonlight with criminal action; some criminals are leveraged for state goals. China, Iran, North Korea, and Russia often rely on criminals, technology firms, or other nonstate proxies to conduct attacks. During the war between Russia and Ukraine, criminal groups, hacktivists, and a group of Ukrainian citizens calling themselves the IT Army conducted distributed denial of service, ransomware, and data breach hacks in support of both sides. Hacktivists dumped Russian emails, passwords,

Figure 2. CYBER OPERATIONS TAKE SEVERAL FORMS

Distributed Denial of Service

The intentional paralyzing of a computer network by flooding it with data sent simultaneously from many individual computers.

Espionage

The act of obtaining confidential information without the information holder's consent.

Data Destruction

The use of malicious software to destroy data on a computer or to render a computer inoperable.

Defacement

The unauthorized act of changing the appearance of a website or social media account.

Sabotage

The use of malware that causes a disruption to a physical process, such as the provision of electricity or normal function of nuclear centrifuges.

Doxing

The act of searching and publishing private or identifying information about an individual or group on the internet, typically with malicious intent.

Financial Theft

The theft of assets, such as cryptocurrencies or cash, for financial gain.

Source: CFR Cyber Operations Tracker.

and other sensitive data on public websites. The Ukrainian government used Twitter to share a list of Russian and Belarusian targets.[8] Criminal hacking could be preparing for, or transitioning to, more destructive attacks. Therefore, a state's willingness to manage cyber activity emanating from its territory will be a significant marker of its commitment to international efforts to secure cyberspace.

In addition, private companies are creating spyware that enables states that cannot create their own cyber capabilities to conduct high-end cyberattacks. Countries can thus not only conduct nation-state-level attacks, but also—if their commitment to the rule of law is weak—target journalists, activists, dissidents, and opposition politicians. An Israeli company, NSO Group Technologies, created malware known as Pegasus that illustrates the multiple uses of these capabilities. Pegasus was reportedly used by law enforcement agencies to capture drug lords, thwart terrorist plots, and fight organized crime. It was allegedly also deployed against civil rights activists in the United Arab Emirates, journalists in Hungary and Poland, and politicians in India and Spain.[9]

Much of the response to these threats has justifiably focused on domestic policy and improving the defense and resilience of government and private-sector networks. Since the Bill Clinton administration, policymakers and legislators have attempted to improve information sharing between the public and private sectors, define authorities and build cyber capacity in the federal government, and raise security standards in critical infrastructure networks. The Cyberspace Solarium Commission, established by the 2019 National Defense Authorization Act (NDAA), offered more than eighty recommendations as part of a strategy of "layered cyber deterrence." Twenty-five of the commission's recommendations have been codified into law, including the establishment of a Senate-confirmed national cyber director within the Executive Office of the President.[10] In March 2022, President Joe Biden signed legislation mandating critical infrastructure owners to report within seventy-two hours if they were hacked or within twenty-four hours if they made a ransomware payment.[11]

Less attention has been paid to rethinking a vision of U.S. foreign policy for cyberspace that contends with a fragmented, insecure internet and its accelerating weaponization. The United States has tried to set the rules of the road using a combination of international norms, "naming and shaming," indictments, and sanctions. Despite agreement at the United Nations on some of the norms of responsible state behavior, these efforts have so far had little influence on Chinese, Iranian, North Korean, or Russian cyber operations. Deterrence of cyberattacks below the threshold of use of force or armed attack—most attacks—has failed. As a result, the United States has adopted a doctrine of persistent engagement and forward defense, based on disrupting attackers before they reach U.S. networks.

The United States is at an inflection point: the risks in cyberspace are growing, and incumbent strategies are not working.

The increased instability of cyberspace presents a grave challenge. Compared with its adversaries, the United States stands largely alone, the most connected society but with the most vulnerable data. Washington needs a comprehensive digital, cyber, and foreign policy strategy that confronts the reality of the end of the global internet. Moving slowly will result in not only the continued deterioration of U.S. security and economic interests but also a failure to capture fully the benefits of the next wave of digital innovation.

The United States is at an inflection point: the risks in cyberspace are growing, and incumbent strategies are not working. A cyber policy grounded in reality has three pillars.

First, Washington should consolidate a coalition of allies and friends around a vision of the internet that preserves—to the greatest degree possible—a trusted, protected international communication platform. This would not be an alliance of democracies, but rather a digital architecture that promotes the trusted flow of data and transparent international standards. The United States should work with allies and partners to develop international rules and agreements governing how the public and private sectors collect, use, protect, store, and share data. Washington should promote regional digital trade negotiations and adopt a shared policy on digital privacy that is interoperable with Europe's GDPR. This coalition of trusted states should build an international cybercrime center, support capacity development in developing economies, and cooperate on technological innovation in sectors critical to offensive and defensive cyber operations.

Second, the United States should balance more targeted diplomatic and economic pressure on adversaries, as well as more disruptive cyber operations, with clear statements about self-imposed restraint on specific types of targets agreed to among U.S. allies. Such statements would include limitations on destructive and disruptive attacks on state financial and electoral systems, as well as negotiations with Beijing and Moscow on the threats to strategic stability caused by cyberattacks on NC3 systems. By limiting the risk of misperception and miscalculation among nuclear powers, these restraints are in the United States' interest because they would reduce the likelihood of catastrophic outcomes. The United States and its partners should also develop coalition-wide practices for disclosing vulnerabilities and applying pressure on states that deliberately provide cybercriminal safe havens.

Third, the United States needs to get its domestic house in order. Digital competition is essential to future strategic and economic interests and should be prioritized in national security strategies. Intelligence agencies should be tasked for cybersecurity risks, and the dangers in domestic cyberspace diminished by incentivizing ISPs to identify and reduce malicious activities occurring on or through their infrastructure. Washington should promote the flow of cybersecurity talent among coalition partners and develop the expertise needed to conduct U.S. cyber foreign policy.

The United States needs to move urgently on cyber and digital competition. Failing to act will significantly harm U.S. security and economic interests in the future.

FINDINGS

A Divided Internet

From the earliest days of the ARPANET through the 1990s, the United States shaped the development of the internet to conform with both its national interests and its unique global image. For the last two decades, the United States continued to promote its vision of a single, open, interoperable, secure, and reliable global network, even as much of the world began to push back against this ideal. In theory, the internet, known in the 1990s as "the information superhighway," should have had a liberalizing effect on world politics as countries around the world connected to the network and Western ideas flowed without the filter of government control.[12]

U.S. officials and technologists often presented the internet as a take-it-or-leave-it proposition: governments would either plug in, allow the free flow of data, and enjoy the growth and prosperity of the digital age, or opt out and disadvantage themselves economically and politically. U.S. Secretary of State Hillary Clinton warned in a 2010 speech that "countries that restrict free access to information or violate the basic rights of internet users risk walling themselves off from the progress of the next century."[13]

The era of the global internet is over.

Yet from the beginning, many governments—including Washington's close allies—rejected this vision of a benign internet. Owing to their histories with antisemitism and different approaches to freedom of speech and the press, France and Germany, for example, demanded that U.S. platforms censor Nazi speech and refrain from selling or displaying banned materials such as Adolf Hitler's infamous autobiographical work *Mein Kampf*. Those early demands produced the geo-located internet in operation today, in which the content seen and the products offered are determined by where an IP address is physically located on the globe.

The 2013 disclosures of U.S. intelligence collection by National Security Agency (NSA) contractor Edward Snowden raised suspicion in many European countries about the risks of dependence on American information and communication technologies. In 2016, the EU adopted the General Data Protection Regulation, which enhanced individual control over private data. The regulation has become a model for data privacy laws in Brazil, Japan, South Africa, South Korea, and other countries. Two rulings by the Court of Justice of the European Union (CJEU), Schrems I and Schrems II, invalidated the EU-U.S. Privacy Shield framework, an agreement that allowed U.S. firms to transfer the data of European citizens, stating that it did not adequately protect EU citizen data from the potential surveillance of U.S. law enforcement and intelligence agencies (see figure 3).[14]

Although the GDPR allows Europe to influence the global debate over data governance, some European leaders also have argued for greater technological autonomy from Chinese hardware and U.S. software and infrastructure. In September 2021, for example, the European Commission announced plans to introduce legislation to promote semiconductor self-sufficiency. Europe is working to promote alternatives to Amazon, Google, Meta, and Microsoft through projects such as Gaia-X, a European shared cloud infrastructure.[15] In early 2022, while holding its six-month rotating presidency of the EU Council, France identified EU digital sovereignty as one of three priorities. Privacy and security regulations could be used to require organizations to work with EU-controlled companies favored by the EU digital sovereignty policies. The war in Ukraine is an impetus for closer transatlantic cooperation, but it has also reinforced the arguments for European tech sovereignty, with the European Council declaring in March 2022 the need to "take further decisive steps towards building our European sovereignty, reducing our dependencies, and designing a new growth and investment model."[16]

China and other authoritarian regimes deployed alternatives to the U.S. model even more forcefully. They see the open internet and

Figure 3. COUNTRIES DIFFER ON DATA LOCALIZATION LAW

Number of regulations by country as of July 2021

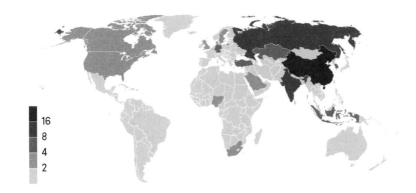

16
8
4
2

Notes: Data localization refers to restrictions placed on the ability of companies to move, store, process, or otherwise handle users' personal data. Numbers include explicit and de facto regulations.

Source: Information Technology and Innovation Foundation.

U.S. tech companies as instruments of regime change. Over time, the Chinese government developed the technical and regulatory capabilities to actively censor the internet traffic that enters and leaves its country, rapidly take down information and block collective action, and tightly surveil, harass, and, when necessary, detain users. Platforms operating in China are legally responsible for content on their sites and employ legions of monitors to block and report activity of which the state disapproves.[17]

Russia's internet was once more open and freewheeling. But after street protests in Moscow in 2012, the government began more actively blacklisting, censoring, and blocking content. Russia's internet regulator, Roskomnadzor, ramped up its demands on Apple, Twitter, and other American companies to remove online content it deems illegal or to restore pro-Kremlin material that has been blocked. Russian President Vladimir Putin is also looking to decouple the domestic internet, Runet, from the global internet, moving users from American platforms to Russian social media and search engines.

In 2019, Russia adopted the Sovereign Internet Law, which seeks to shield its Runet from foreign attacks and mandates annual tests of telecommunications ability to disconnect the domestic internet from global cyberspace. During the Russian invasion of Ukraine, after Facebook announced that it would fact check claims from state media, Moscow entirely blocked the social media platform. It went on to block other sites as well, forcing Russians who wanted access to information not censored by Moscow to rely on virtual private networks (VPNs).[18]

Authoritarian regimes are not alone in seeking to tame the online world. Domestic and foreign actors' use of social media to spread disinformation, misinformation, hate speech, and violent and extremist content has made policymakers in many democracies increasingly wary of an unregulated internet. For example, Germany's NetzDG, or the Network Enforcement Act, levies fines of up to €50 million for failure to take down "evidently criminal" content within twenty-four hours. Singapore's Protection From Online Falsehoods and Manipulation Act requires online platforms to issue corrections or remove content that the government deems false.[19]

When they cannot filter content at scale, countries can simply decide to disconnect briefly from the internet. Sixty nations have temporarily turned off the internet more than nine hundred times altogether over the last seven years.[20] India, the world's largest democracy, is also the world leader in internet shutdowns. In 2019 and 2020, Indian officials suspended the internet as many as 164 times for over 13,000 hours.[21] Over the last three years, Ethiopia, Niger, Nigeria, and Uganda have also used shutdowns to control information and influence elections.

Despite the continued splintering of the internet, hundreds of millions of users of the network regard it as indispensable to their daily lives and to the operations of their geographically dispersed businesses. These needs and expectations of the internet as a connective platform have only increased since the beginning of COVID-19.

In addition, advanced economies are at the cusp of a new wave of digital innovation. Proponents of blockchain technology argue that Web 3.0 will be more secure, inclusive, and resilient, giving users greater control of their data and privacy. Blockchain technologies are expected to contribute $1.76 trillion to the global economy by 2030.[22] The metaverse, as some describe it, is a linked virtual world that is an extension of the physical world, which could become a persistent, immersive, three-dimensional (3-D) reality in which people play, work, and socialize. The Internet of Things, which envisions tens of billions of internet-connected devices, is becoming the backbone of smart homes and cities that increase safety, improve health, and conserve energy. The consulting company McKinsey & Company estimates that

IoT devices could enable \$5.5 trillion to \$12.6 trillion in value globally by 2030.[23]

If networks are built and operated for the needs of national sovereignty rather than to achieve global scale, then policymakers will need to understand and address the accompanying unavailability of information required to make business or personal decisions, the impaired ability to scale innovation at the lowest possible cost, and the ripple effects of digital fragmentation across other aspects of bilateral and multilateral relationships.

U.S. policies promoting an open, global internet have failed.

From the George W. Bush administration through the end of Donald Trump's presidency, the United States promoted what is broadly known as the "internet freedom agenda." This mandate was both economic, calling for a relatively laissez faire approach to regulation, and political, promoting an American ideal of free speech on the internet. In 2006, for example, the Bush administration established the Global Internet Freedom Task Force to maximize the free flow of data and funded grants for circumventing censorship. The Barack Obama administration had its own NetFreedom Task Force and spent over \$100 million on encryption and anti-censorship technologies.[24]

Yet the United States has been unable to counter the persistent advance of the concept of cyber sovereignty. Beijing is sharing its technology and experience with other countries, holding meetings and seminars on its model of internet control with at least thirty countries and providing technical assistance to more than a dozen. In 2015, for example, Tanzania passed cybersecurity laws that resembled China's. Egypt, Laos, Pakistan, Uganda, Vietnam, and Zimbabwe have proposed or passed legislation that mimics the blocking of websites, real name registration, data sharing, and content takedowns that characterize Chinese regulations. Early in 2021, Cambodia adopted Chinese-style internet controls and created an internet gateway through which all web traffic is routed and monitored.[25]

Beijing and Moscow are collaborating to reshape the global internet and reduce U.S. influence. In 2015, Chinese President Xi Jinping and Putin signed an agreement "on cooperation in ensuring international information security." In the years after its signing, the majority of exchanges appear to be designed to share technologies, information, and processes on the control of the internet. The two countries have also promoted cyber sovereignty through the United Nations, International Telecommunication Union, Shanghai Cooperation Organization, and the BRICS group (Brazil, Russia, India, China, and South Africa).[26]

Even as the free and open internet loses ground, the United States and Europe remain divided over the legitimate role of privacy, antitrust, industry promotion, and data localization regulations. Despite a shared assessment of the threat of Chinese and Russian cyber operations and a commitment to the protection of human rights online, these unresolved issues have made it difficult to present a common front. Moreover, a number of democracies and more open societies have pursued new rules for technology companies on content, data, and competition, which has often resulted in limits of free expression and greater access to private data by government agencies.

In an effort to turn this tide, in April 2022 the Biden administration along with sixty-one countries issued a Declaration for the Future of the Internet.[27] The signatories committed themselves to supporting "a future for the Internet that is an [sic] open, free, global, interoperable, reliable, and secure," as well as to protecting human rights online, securing individuals' privacy, and maintaining secure and reliable connectivity. The declaration reaffirms a positive vision of a "single interconnected communications system for all of humanity" that fosters innovation and economic growth, promotes creativity, reinforces democratic governance, and provides unfettered access to knowledge.

The driving idea behind the declaration is correct. Simply opposing the Chinese and Russian models of the internet is not enough. The United States needs to mobilize partners around a proactive vision of what it desires to accomplish in cyberspace, but the declaration has no binding commitments or new policy initiatives. Nothing suggests that this time is different and that a statement of strong principles will be able to stop or reverse the trend toward fragmentation. The United States needs to develop a path forward based on the reality of the internet today.

Data is a source of geopolitical power and competition.

Data is an indisputable source of national power. It fuels innovation, economic growth, and national security. It is at the center of global trade, with cross-border data flows growing roughly 112 times over from 2008 to 2020.[28] The rapid expansion of fifth-generation (5G) wireless networks, cloud computing, and the Internet of Things means an explosion of data. The total data generated by 2025 is set to accelerate exponentially to 175 zettabytes; and this data will generate innovations in agriculture, logistics, manufacturing, pharmaceuticals, and other critical sectors.[29] The World Economic Forum projects that 70 percent of new value created in the economy over the next decade will be based on digitally enabled platform business models.[30] Technology companies that collect, analyze, and commercialize data, such as Alibaba, Alphabet, Amazon, Meta, and Tencent, have replaced oil and gas producers, consumer goods, and financial institutions at the top of the list of the world's most valuable firms.

Data is also central to national security. Advances in machine learning, data analytics, and other digital technologies have a significant effect on military and intelligence capabilities. The National Security Commission on Artificial Intelligence warned that the U.S. military's technical advantage could be lost within the next decade without an accelerated adoption of artificial intelligence, warning that "AI-enhanced capabilities will be the tools of first resort in a new era of conflict as strategic competitors develop AI concepts and technologies for military and other malign uses and cheap and commercially available AI applications ranging from 'deepfakes' to lethal drones become available to rogue states, terrorists, and criminals."[31] National intelligence agencies can collect and analyze data at scale, but new technologies also enable nonstate actors and individuals to execute the same tasks, sometimes more quickly than governments.[32]

U.S. adversaries increasingly see data as central to their economic and national security and are developing national strategies for its collection, application, and protection. China hosts the world's largest e-commerce market, boasting 40 percent of global sales, and introduced the world's first state-sponsored digital currency.[33] In April 2020, China's State Council formally designated data as a factor of production, joining land, labor, capital, and technology. In a 2021 speech to a Chinese Communist Party Politburo study session, Xi declared the digital economy to be a "critical force in reorganizing global factor resources, reshaping global economic structures, and changing global competition structures."[34] National Security Advisor Jake Sullivan remarked, "Strategic competitors see big data as a strategic asset."[35] So should the United States.

The United States has taken itself out of the game on digital trade.

Deep domestic political divides limit the United States' ability to lead internationally. Despite countless congressional hearings on the benefits and drawbacks of regulating data markets and technology companies, the continued failure to adopt comprehensive privacy and data protection rules at home undercuts Washington's argument that it has a model worth emulating. The United States is highly polarized on issues of free speech and the threats of market consolidation and as a result has been unable to decide on which values to optimize. This sense of inefficacy is heightened in contrast to the speed with which China has rolled out a matrix of regulations that includes the national cybersecurity law, data security law, and personal information protection law.[36] Nowhere has domestic policy harmed the U.S. ability to lead more than in the arena of digital trade, the cross-border flow of data and digital services that now accounts for nearly $3 trillion in global wealth.

The U.S. withdrawal from the Trans-Pacific Partnership and continued aversion to multilateral trade agreements severely limit its ability to shape the rules guiding digital trade. Although the digital chapters of the U.S.-Korea Free Trade Agreement (KORUS) and the U.S.-Mexico-Canada Agreement (USMCA), as well as the U.S.-Japan Digital Trade Agreement, have strong protections for cross-border data flows, the United States has been sidelined as other trade groups come together. The Regional Comprehensive Economic Partnership (RCEP), an agreement among fifteen countries in the Asia-Pacific, for example, represents 30 percent of global gross domestic product (GDP) and entered into force without the United States on January 1, 2022. RCEP's provisions regarding data localization, restrictions on cross-border data flows, and policies that champion domestic industry are, however, weak.[37]

Beijing has recently submitted its application to accede to the Comprehensive and Progressive Agreement for Trans-Pacific Partnership and to join the Digital Economy Partnership Agreement. The Biden administration has announced that it is developing an Indo-Pacific framework that will address digital technology, along with other issues, but no further details have been released.[38]

Rising Risks in Cyberspace

Much of the early concern around cyberspace focused on disruptive and destructive attacks on critical infrastructure. In 2007, Russia-based hackers mounted a high-intensity, low-sophistication attack on Estonia over a dispute about the movement of a statue of a Russian soldier commemorating World War II. That campaign, which some dubbed Web War I, severely disrupted banking, media, and public services. In 2012, General Keith Alexander, director of the National Security Agency, said in congressional testimony that it was only a matter of time before hackers destroyed elements of critical infrastructure in the United States. The same year, in a speech to business executives, then U.S. Secretary of Defense and former CIA Director Leon Panetta cautioned that the country could face a "cyber Pearl Harbor" and warned that a terrorist group or enemy state could gain control of "critical switches" to "derail passenger trains, or even more dangerous, derail trains loaded with lethal chemicals."[39]

In a joint operation, the United States and Israel appeared to be the first to cross the Rubicon, launching the first known cyber campaign to cause physical damage. "Olympic Games" was designed to set Iran's nuclear program back by destroying centrifuges at its enrichment facility in Natanz. In response, Iranian hackers knocked offline the websites of a number of American banks, including Wells Fargo, JPMorgan Chase, and Bank of America. In 2012, Iran wiped the data on thirty thousand computers at oil producer Saudi Aramco, and a follow-on attack damaged Rasgas, a joint venture between Qatar Petroleum and ExxonMobil that is the second-biggest producer of liquefied natural gas in the world. North Korean hackers disrupted South Korean banks and telecommunications and, in anger over a film that mocked North Korean leader Kim Jong-un, stole one hundred terabytes of internal data from Sony and damaged two-thirds of the company's servers and computers.[40]

These types of attacks were, however, the exceptions. Over the last decade, most cyber operations have been attacks that violate sovereignty but remain below the threshold for the use of force or armed attack (see figure 4). These breaches are used for political advantage, espionage, and international statecraft, with the most damaging attacks undermining trust and confidence in social, political, and economic institutions.[41]

Russian operatives skilled in cyber espionage interfered in the Ukrainian election of 2014 through a combination of hacking, disinformation, and denial of service attacks. Moscow used a similar playbook in the 2016 U.S. elections, breaking into the email accounts of the Democratic National Committee and Clinton campaign chairman John Podesta and posting the documents publicly. These documents, as well as disinformation and misinformation that exacerbated social, cultural, and political divisions, were amplified on social media through bots and fake accounts. Russia continues to develop and evolve these methods, posing challenges to the cohesion of the United States and its allies.[42]

China-backed hackers deployed widespread political and military espionage as well as a massive campaign of cyber-enabled intellectual property theft from the private sector. Chinese operatives targeted the State Department, U.S. Department of Defense, White House, and defense contractors and, in 2015, were behind the theft of twenty-two million records of federal employees, including their security background checks, from the Office of Personnel Management. Cyber espionage has also been central to Beijing's attempt to make the Chinese economy more competitive and less dependent on foreign suppliers for critical technologies. The Office of the National Counterintelligence Executive declared that "Chinese actors are the world's most active and persistent perpetrators of economic espionage."[43] Chinese operators have become adept at targeting and exploiting big data, which can be used for intelligence and counterintelligence as well as driving advancements in machine learning.

Over the last few years, Chinese and Russian operations have become more brazen and proficient. Chinese hackers exploited a so-called zero-day vulnerability—a software weakness unknown to its vendor—in Microsoft Exchange email servers, allowing them to gain access to thousands of sensitive networks. Moreover, knowing that Microsoft was pushing out a protective patch for the vulnerability,

Figure 4. U.S. ADVERSARIES ARE SPONSORING CYBERATTACKS

Number of suspected state-sponsored cyber operations from 2005 to 2021, selected countries

Sponsor	Espionage	Financial theft	Sabotage, denial of service, and other
China	152	0	4
Russia	87	0	23
Iran	44	1	10
North Korea	38	9	7

Note: Data is based primarily on publicly available, English-language reports.

Source: CFR Cyber Operations Tracker.

the hackers scanned almost the entire internet to find exposed servers to be compromised.[44] The breach of the software firm SolarWinds allowed Russian hackers to access the networks of major government agencies and over one hundred companies (see figure 5). The SolarWinds campaign was exposed because the cybersecurity firm FireEye discovered hackers in their networks, stealing "Red Team" tools, a collection of malware and exploits used to test customers' vulnerabilities.

The trend line thus far is clear: increased digitization goes hand in hand with increased vulnerability, given that nearly every aspect of business and statecraft becomes exposed to disruption, theft, or manipulation.

Cybercrime is a national security risk.

COVID-19 has accelerated global dependence on digital infrastructure. Public health measures and stay-at-home orders led to a massive shift in teleworking. By the end of 2020, 71 percent of workers in the United States had switched in whole or in part to working from remote

Figure 5. ONCE DISCOVERED, SOLARWINDS HACK LED TO SWIFT U.S. RESPONSE

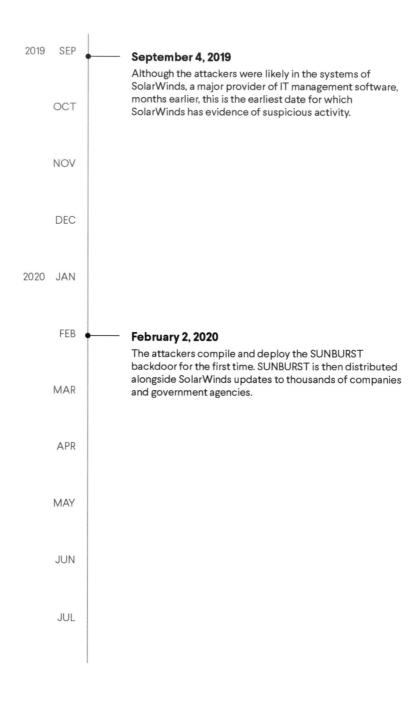

September 4, 2019
Although the attackers were likely in the systems of SolarWinds, a major provider of IT management software, months earlier, this is the earliest date for which SolarWinds has evidence of suspicious activity.

February 2, 2020
The attackers compile and deploy the SUNBURST backdoor for the first time. SUNBURST is then distributed alongside SolarWinds updates to thousands of companies and government agencies.

Continued

AUG

SEP

OCT

NOV

DEC

2021 JAN

FEB

MAR

APR

MAY

December 13, 2020

FireEye, a major U.S. cybersecurity company, announces that it was compromised through SolarWinds and identifies numerous government agencies and private companies that were also compromised, including the U.S. Departments of Commerce and Homeland Security. The Cybersecurity and Infrastructure Security Agency (CISA) releases an emergency directive and orders federal agencies to shut down SolarWinds products.

January 5, 2021

The United States formally attributes the hack to Russian intelligence services and reveals the scale of the attack, with over 18,000 companies and organizations compromised, although not all compromised companies' systems were accessed.

February 22, 2021

Congress convenes a multiday hearing on the SolarWinds attack. The next day, Microsoft executives testify that the SolarWinds attackers had accessed the company's source code but had not made any changes.

March 7, 2021

U.S. officials claim U.S. intelligence agencies have planned a series of retaliatory attacks against Russian government technology infrastructure. The attacks are reportedly meant to be visible to Russian intelligence agencies and are part of President Biden's stronger response to cyberattacks.

April 15, 2021

The United States imposes sanctions on Russia for the SolarWinds hack and other "destabilizing international actions." The sanctions target Russia's financial system and technology companies, along with specific individuals believed to be involved in the attack.

Source: SolarWinds; Mandiant; White House; CFR research.

locations outside their offices. COVID-related cyber operations surged, with hackers targeting vaccine research and development (R&D) efforts. The swell of online activities increased the incentives for malicious actors to exploit vulnerabilities in all sectors of economic and political activity.[45]

Over the last three years, the risk of ransomware has ballooned (see figure 6). The risk is not just financial. Ransomware attacks have paralyzed local governments, school districts, and hospitals. In 2019, a ransomware attack shut down the operations of a U.S. Coast Guard facility for thirty hours, and the University of Vermont Medical Center furloughed or reassigned about three hundred employees after an attack on the hospital's networks. Homeland Security officials worried that ransomware attacks on voter registration systems could disrupt the 2020 elections. In May 2022, the new president of Costa Rica, Rodrigo Chaves Robles, declared a national emergency after a ransomware attack by the Conti gang crippled the Finance and Labor Ministry as well as the customs agency. The group also posted stolen files to the dark web to extort the government to pay the ransom.[46]

Ransomware groups are professionalizing and marketing in ways reminiscent of Silicon Valley startups. Highly capable groups have become "initial access brokers" that specialize in gaining a foothold on target networks and then selling that access to ransomware operators who can rent a payload—a separate encryption malware—from a "ransomware-as-a-service" provider.[47] Zero days are expensive to buy and develop. They have historically been deployed by state-backed groups, yet in 2021 one-third of all hacking groups exploiting zero days were financially motivated criminals.[48] With greater ransom payments, criminal hacking groups can recruit and pay for technical talent. The most elite groups are developing skills previously reserved for a small number of military and intelligence agencies, but "crime-as-a-service" providers offer a wide range of attacks with a significant economic effect.

The emergence of cryptocurrencies has enabled this explosive growth in cybercrime. Ransomware preexisted cryptocurrencies, yet criminals struggled to extract significant payments through the traditional financial system. Cryptocurrencies make it easier to monetize breaches in network security; as a result, more groups are forming to launch ransomware. According to Chainalysis, a cryptocurrency tracking and analytics firm, in 2021 more than $400 million worth of cryptocurrency payments went to groups "highly likely to be affiliated with Russia."[49] The United States has passed

Figure 6. CYBERCRIME RANSOM PAYMENTS ARE RISING

Total value of ransomware-related payments, based on reports by U.S. financial institutions

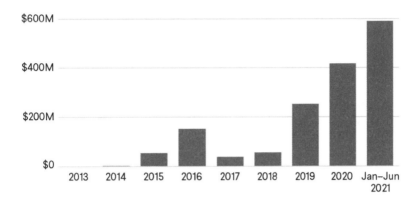

Note: The number for 2021 reflects only the first six months of the year. Numbers are the total value of suspicious activity reported by U.S. financial institutions in ransomware-related Suspicious Activity Reports. Dollar figures are calculated based on the value of bitcoin at the time of transaction.

Source: U.S. Treasury Department Financial Crimes Enforcement Network.

"know-your-customer" provisions for cryptocurrency exchanges and sanctioned Russian exchanges, and in June 2021 the FBI tracked and "clawed back" a portion of the payment made in bitcoin to the Darkside ransomware group that extorted Colonial Pipeline. Whether these efforts are sustainable or can change the economics of ransomware is unclear.[50]

In addition, authoritarian states have increasingly blurred the line between state and nonstate actors in cyberspace. The United States has alleged that China, Iran, North Korea, and Russia at times rely on private technology firms, organized crime and hacker groups, and civil militias to conduct operations. During the Russia-Ukraine war, the Conti group published a statement declaring their loyalty to Moscow and threatening retaliation against countries that supported Ukraine.[51] As Mieke Eoyang, the U.S. deputy assistant secretary of defense for cyber policy, told the House Armed Services Committee, "The line between nation-state and criminal actors is increasingly blurry as nation-states turn to criminal proxies as a tool of state power, then turn a blind eye to the cybercrime perpetrated by the same malicious actors."[52]

> The United States can no longer treat cyber and information operations as two separate domains.

Although disinformation, misinformation, and the abuse of social media are outside the scope of this Task Force, the Russia-Ukraine war demonstrates how tightly intertwined cyber and information operations are. Ukraine, with the assistance of the United States and its European partners, was able in the first months of the conflict to defend its critical infrastructure from disruptive cyberattacks. Continued access to communication and internet networks proved crucial to Ukrainian President Volodymyr Zelensky and other officials' mobilizing domestic and international support for Ukraine, controlling the narrative of the war, and countering Russian propaganda. On the other side, Russian hackers planted a fake message in the livestream of a broadcast announcing a surrender and broke into the Facebook accounts of high-profile Ukrainian military leaders and politicians, then used their access to post false messages that Ukrainian forces were laying down their arms.[53]

The United States has historically separated cyber and information security, but American adversaries have traditionally not distinguished between the two. In their view, the confidentiality, integrity, and assurance of computer networks are integral—and in some sense subordinate—to the battle over information spaces, and cyberattacks enabled significant capabilities in information operations. Numerous Russian documents and strategies describe cyber operations as integral to information security. After the creation of U.S. Cyber Command (CYBERCOM), at a meeting of Russian and U.S. defense officials, one Russian officer reportedly derided the lack of information warfare in Cyber Command's mission. General Nikolai Makarov told his counterparts, "One uses information to destroy nations, not networks."[54]

Although the United States has struggled both to counter information operations at home and to find the right authorities and institutions to promote its efforts to shape narratives in cyberspace, the Russia-Ukraine war has clearly demonstrated how cyber capabilities, defensive and offensive, are essential enablers of successful information operations. Remarking on the conflict, Lieutenant General Charles Moore, CYBERCOM deputy commander, noted, "Without a doubt, what we have learned is that cyber-effects operations in conjunction— in more of a combined arms approach—with what we call traditionally information operations, is an extremely powerful tool."[55]

AI and other new technologies will increase strategic instability.

The consensus in the cybersecurity community is that the offense has the advantage over the defense, but this is less true for complex, destructive attacks. Only the most sophisticated attackers can maintain an undetected presence on networks over an extended period. It is difficult for the attacker to create widespread, long-lasting effects, and sophisticated attacks require a significant investment of resources and talent.[56]

The relationship between attackers and defenders could shift, however, as new technologies come online. The rapid rise of artificial intelligence and, eventually, quantum computing could make the work of cyber defenders more difficult over time, with faster and faster computers enabling increasingly complex attacks and more rapid network intrusion. AI-enabled state cyberattacks would be more precise and tailored; the rise of sophisticated natural language processing models is likely to improve spear-phishing abilities. Malware could mutate into thousands of forms once it is in a network. For the defender, AI could accelerate the detection of attackers inside a network. Machine learning could help automate vulnerability discovery, deception, and attack disruption.[57]

The eventual effect of such developments on the dynamic between offense and defense is uncertain. One outcome that appears likely is that both attackers and defenders will rely on a greater degree of automation, which could have an adverse effect on strategic stability. The United States now exerts tight political control over state-sponsored cyber operations. A reliance on a higher degree of automation could lead to unintended consequences.

A Failure to Impose Costs

The United States has failed to impose sufficient costs on attackers.

Scholars and policymakers have long debated whether deterrence is possible in cyberspace. Early works argued that several characteristics of cyberspace made it nearly impossible to dissuade a potential adversary from taking a hostile action with the threat of retaliation or a response that imposes unacceptable costs.[58] One of the central problems with deterring computer attacks is retaliating in a timely, accurate, and proportional manner. As noted earlier, most attacks appear to be below the threshold for meaningful military retaliation. Deterrence by denial, which would raise the cost to attackers by improving defense, is equally difficult, as the defender seems to be at a perpetual disadvantage.

In addition, skeptics of deterrence highlight the interconnected nature of cyberspace, technological changes that shift the battlespace, and the near constant contact between adversaries to argue that cyber actors will constantly seek advantages in cyberspace.[59] Skeptics argue that, rather than holding on to the hope of deterring actions, the United States should adopt a posture that encompasses resilience, active defense, and more aggressive disruption of attackers.

The proponents of cyber deterrence agree with critics that Cold War or classical nuclear deterrence does not cohere in cyberspace. Cyber deterrence in their view is less an attempt to prevent one clear catastrophic event, such as a nuclear strike, and more a series of efforts to shape behavior along a spectrum of possible attacks.[60] In this view, deterrence could fend off destructive attacks on the U.S. transportation, energy, or electrical networks. Few actors are capable of launching such attacks, these actions are clearly above the threshold for an armed attack, and the United States would likely be able to determine who is responsible and launch a punishing reprisal.

For other types of attacks, such as cybercrime or espionage, the supporters of cyber deterrence argue that the United States cannot expect a complete cessation of activity. Instead, it will have to adopt a layered approach that blends threats of punishment, denial, sanctions, diplomatic efforts, economic entanglement, and norms, as well as the disruption of persistent engagement.[61] A layered approach could allow the United States to achieve pauses, cessations, or restraints on certain classes of cyberattacks.

Both strains of thought have influenced U.S. cyber strategy. In 2018, U.S. Cyber Command released a strategic vision announcing the concept of persistent engagement,[62] Cyber Command would maintain "the initiative in cyberspace by continuously engaging and contesting adversaries and causing them uncertainty wherever they maneuver." Or, as General Paul Nakasone, commander of CYBERCOM, wrote about the implementation of the strategy, "To protect our most critical public and private institutions from threats that continue to evolve in cyberspace, we cannot operate episodically. While we cannot ignore vital cyber defense missions, we must take this fight to the enemy, just as we do in other aspects of conflict."[63]

To enable this strategy, the Trump administration relaxed restrictions on offensive cyber actions. National Security Presidential Memorandum 13 reportedly allowed Cyber Command to undertake actions that fall below the use of force or that would not cause death, destruction, or significant economic upheaval without a lengthy approval process.[64]

Provisions in the John McCain Act (2019 NDAA) preauthorize CYBERCOM to take "appropriate and proportional" action in foreign cyberspace to "disrupt, defeat, and deter" an "active, systematic, and ongoing" campaign of attacks on government or private networks by China, Iran, North Korea, or Russia.[65] The Trump administration also reportedly issued a presidential finding allowing the CIA more freedom to conduct offensive cyber operations.[66]

Since the announcement of the strategy, Cyber Command, working with the NSA, actively protected the 2018 election, disrupting the Internet Research Agency and other Russian actors. CYBERCOM has also deployed personnel to launch "hunt forward" missions in sixteen countries, including Estonia, Lithuania, Montenegro, and North Macedonia, as well as countries in Asia and the Middle East, to monitor adversary activities and identify malware and share it with U.S. partners.[67] Cyber Command worked with an unnamed foreign government in 2021 to interrupt the operation of the ransomware gang REvil, allegedly blocking its website by hijacking traffic.[68] In January 2022, the United States posted tools used by MuddyWater, a group with suspected ties to the Iranian Ministry of Intelligence and Security, to VirusTotal, a public repository of malware. It had previously posted samples of malware used by North Korean and Russian cyber actors.[69] Months before the invasion of Ukraine, cyber mission forces from CYBERCOM deployed to the country to search for Russian malware implanted in critical infrastructure.[70]

Given the high degree of secrecy around cyber operations and the lack of public information on the number of attacks that Cyber Command disrupts, it is difficult to gauge the success of persistent engagement. Trump administration officials have argued that CYBERCOM successfully disrupted Russian information operations during the 2018 elections.[71] These successes appear to be tactical, slowing adversaries for a time. The SolarWinds and Microsoft Exchange Server attacks suggest, however, that the United States continues to fail to impose significant costs on adversaries for cyber espionage operations. The United States' high degree of digital dependency enforces restraint, preventing it from retaliating powerfully against harmful operations in cyberspace. Moving to more destructive attacks threatens an escalatory response by adversaries that could leave the United States more vulnerable. Mutual cyber offense alone is unlikely to function as a sufficiently clear deterrent to opponents.

Norms are more useful in binding friends together than in constraining adversaries.

While the United States has searched for more effective ways to impose costs on attackers, it has also worked to define the rules for responsible state behavior in cyberspace. These efforts have included multilateral and bilateral negotiations as well as public attribution of attacks, indictments, and sanctions.

The United States has pursued norms—expectations about behavior that make it possible to hold other states accountable—because arms control agreements, like those used to control conventional or nuclear weapons, will not prove viable in cyberspace. Nuclear arms agreements counted, monitored, and limited the range and number of air-, sea-, land-, and space-based weapons. In contrast, cyber exploits reflect vulnerabilities in computer code and lack transparency. The certainty of verification does not exist, and as a result, the composition of a stable system of arms control in cyberspace becomes a practical impossibility. Nuclear and conventional weapons take years to produce and deploy to national militaries; cyber weapons, in contrast, are developed more quickly and in relative secrecy. Moreover, only a handful of countries have nuclear weapons. Many more states, along with a handful of nonstate actors, are developing cyber doctrines and corresponding capabilities. Finally, over time nuclear weapons were governed by a norm of stable deterrence and nonuse, whereas cyber operations are difficult to deter and used extensively.[72]

The United States has enjoyed some success gaining consensus on norms through the UN Group of Governmental Experts on Advancing Responsible State Behavior in Cyberspace in the Context of International Security (GGE).[73] First established in 2004, the GGE now consists of experts representing twenty-five countries, including the United States, Australia, China, Russia, and the United Kingdom. In 2015, it issued a consensus report on a set of norms that largely reflected the U.S. delegation's position on the application of international law in cyberspace.[74] Eleven norms were formally adopted by the UN General Assembly, including those of state responsibility and the duty to assist, as well as a prohibition of intentionally damaging or impairing others' critical infrastructures or targeting another state's computer emergency response teams during peacetime.[75]

Follow-on meetings in 2017 failed to reach consensus because the group was divided over how to apply international law. In 2018 Washington and Moscow submitted proposals for parallel processes. The United States pushed for the continuation of the GGE; Russia advocated for an Open-Ended Working Group (OEWG) intended to run through 2025 in which all UN member states could participate. Despite fears that the two groups would diverge in their work, the OEWG issued a report that reaffirmed the 2015 GGE consensus.[76] A joint resolution proposed by the United States and the Russian Federation endorsed both reports, but meetings in the wake of the Russian war on Ukraine have been contentious, with the United States and its allies calling out Russia for violating the norms against interfering with critical infrastructure.

During the Obama administration, in response to a massive cyber campaign by state-backed hackers from China, the United States worked to establish a norm against the cyber-enabled theft of intellectual property in pursuit of competitive economic advantage. This was not a norm shared by all partners. Some U.S. allies were known to conduct espionage on behalf of individual companies. Still, Washington argued that states could be expected to conduct espionage against political or military targets, but operations against the private sector for commercial gain should be off limits.

The norms process requires states to be transparent and provide legal justifications for the operations they undertake. Few states have done this, including the United States.

In an effort to change Chinese behavior, U.S. officials began "naming and shaming" China, warning the espionage threatened stability in the bilateral relationship. In May 2014, in a significant escalation of pressure, the U.S. Department of Justice indicted five People's Liberation Army officers for stealing trade secrets from Westinghouse, U.S. Steel, and other companies. In the summer of 2015, before President Xi's first planned state visit to Washington, officials suggested that the United States would sanction Chinese individuals or entities that benefited from cyber theft. Beijing responded by sending a high-level negotiator before the summit, and during Xi's visit the two sides announced that "neither country's government will conduct or knowingly support cyber-enabled theft of intellectual property, including trade secrets or other confidential business information, with the intent of providing competitive advantages to companies or commercial sectors."[77]

In the first year after the visit, the Obama-Xi agreement appeared to be a success. The cybersecurity firm FireEye reported in June 2016 that the number of network compromises by the China-based hacking groups it tracks dropped from sixty in February 2013 to fewer than ten by May 2016. China went on to announce similar agreements with Australia and the United Kingdom, and the norm against intellectual property theft was included in statements from the Group of Twenty (including China, France, and Russia) and Group of Seven in 2015 and 2017.[78]

As in other domains, the process of creating norms in cyberspace is slow, uneven, and uncertain. Washington's efforts with Beijing proved transitory. In December 2018, for example, the U.S. Justice Department indicted two Chinese hackers with ties to the Ministry of State Security (MSS) for breaching managed service providers and more than forty-five technology companies. The cyber campaign, known as Cloud Hopper, exploited vulnerabilities in cloud computing and targeted some of the world's biggest technology firms. Following the indictment, Australia, Canada, Germany, New Zealand, the United Kingdom, and other allies all issued statements backing the U.S. allegations against China and attributing the attack to the MSS.[79]

The United Nations has affirmed the application of international law to cyberspace, but major actors have flouted the norms endorsed by the GGE and OEWG. Russia's tolerance of ransomware gangs, for example, violates the norm of state responsibility, and operations against the power grid in Kyiv in 2015 and 2016 contravene the norm of noninterference with critical infrastructure during peacetime. Moreover, the norms process requires states to be transparent and provide legal justifications for the operations they undertake. Few states have done this, including the United States.

U.S. efforts to define norms around espionage have also suffered from inconsistent messaging. Many of the indictments and sanctions levied on Russia are for political-military espionage operations that Washington had previously suggested are legitimate and that all states would pursue. U.S. officials signaled that SolarWinds crossed a line because of the scope of the attack, the potential to move from espionage to disruption, the "unusual" burden placed on the private sector of mitigating the attack, the risk to the supply chain, and the theft of FireEye's tools.[80] The ultimate targets, however, are believed to have been some two hundred government and industrial entities, all reasonable subjects for intelligence collection. They are the kind of targets on which the United States intelligence community can and should collect intelligence in adversary nations.

> Indictments and sanctions have been ineffective in stopping state-backed hackers.

The United States has used indictments and sanctions to reinforce norms and try to deter and impose costs on hackers (see figure 7). Public attribution delineates which type of operations the United States considers illegitimate. Though the intent of an operation is difficult to determine, as is whether it is an intelligence, defensive, or offensive effort, the U.S. government and private sector actors in the cybersecurity industry have, with years of difficult experience, developed significant visibility into the identity and tradecraft of disparate cyber actors.

Once an attack is publicly attributed, the United States uses indictments and sanctions to impose costs and deter future attacks. The Department of Justice unsealed 24 indictments from 2014 to 2020, with 195 criminal counts against 93 foreign individuals accused of cyber operations at the behest of a state sponsor.[81] Chinese, Iranian, North Korean, Russian, and Syrian hackers have been charged with a variety of crimes, from malicious destructive hacks to the theft of trade secrets and other intellectual property. The United States and its allies, for example, jointly attributed the NotPetya ransomware attack to Russia's military intelligence, the Main Intelligence Directorate (GRU). In October 2020, a federal grand jury indicted six officers for the attacks.[82]

After the Sony hack of 2015, the Obama administration issued Executive Order 13694, which allows the U.S. Department of the Treasury to block the property of individuals and entities involved in cyber-enabled activities that are a "significant threat to the national security, foreign policy, or economic health or financial stability of the United States."[83] The order was amended in December 2016 to allow for sanctions against cyber-enabled election interference. Until May 2021, the Treasury Department issued 311 cyber-related sanctions, most against Russia (141), Iran (112), and North Korea (18).[84] In April

Figure 7. U.S. HAS IMPOSED HUNDREDS OF CYBER SANCTIONS ON RUSSIA AND IRAN

Number of cyber-related sanctions, 2012 to April 2021

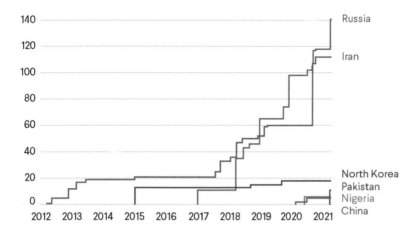

Note: Only countries with five or more sanctions are shown.

Source: U.S. Department of the Treasury, Office of Foreign Assets Control, compiled by Center for a New American Security.

2021, the United States attributed SolarWinds to Russia's Foreign Intelligence Service, and the White House issued an executive order blocking property connected to harmful Russian activities and imposed sanctions on "companies operating in the technology sector of the Russian Federation economy that support Russian Intelligence Services."[85] Although U.S. partners joined in calling out irresponsible behavior, few followed through with indictments or sanctions.

The public attributions, indictments, and sanctions have not imposed significant costs on state-backed hackers. Attributing publicly but lacking either the capability or will to respond effectively makes the United States look hapless and risks inviting more cyberattacks. Few hackers have seen the inside of a U.S. courtroom. As of 2019, of more than fifty indictments since the Obama administration, only five individuals have been arrested for their crimes.[86] Sanctions could have a greater chance of success because they can target individuals and entities of value to policymakers. But so far, Washington has either been unable to identify the right targets or to inflict substantial pain.

Indictments, sanctions, and norms dialogues have been more effective in building coalitions than in deterring or imposing costs on adversaries. These actions—multilateral, explicit, declared, and aspirational—allow Washington to signal to friends and allies what it sees as responsible behavior.

RECOMMENDATIONS

The internet today is more fragmented, less free, and more dangerous than it was at its emergence. The threats in cyberspace continue to grow, and cybercriminals and other proxy actors are a rising challenge to national security. Adversaries are developing comprehensive strategies for cyberspace and making it more difficult for the United States to navigate in a domain of shadows and fierce threats. The United States needs the strategy, the structures, the talent, and the policies for sustained cooperation among the full array of bilateral and multilateral relationships, where digital issues are increasingly important.

A successful marrying of the United States' foreign and cybersecurity policies should be built on three pillars: building a trusted internet coalition based on the free flow of data, balancing more pressure on adversaries with limited norms of restraint on cyber operations, and building capabilities at home.

The first step for the United States is to develop and sustain a coalition of states committed to the trusted flow of data. This will require Washington to reenter regional digital trade negotiations, negotiate with Brussels and others on privacy and government access to data, and offer incentives to other states to join the coalition through an international cybercrime center and cyber development assistance. In support of these efforts, the United States will also need to develop a coalition to promote the security of open-source software and work jointly to retain leadership in technologies critical to cyber strategy, such as AI, semiconductors, and quantum information sciences.

Build a Trusted, Protected Internet Coalition

The United States can do little to prevent authoritarian regimes from creating a separate network that reflects their values. It can, however, preserve and extend the economic and political values of an open internet among a self-selecting coalition. In addition, the United States and its allies will need to address security threats and provide economic and political inducements for states ambivalent about the costs and benefits of allowing a relatively free flow of data.

Although many efforts are underway to bring together a consortium of partners that value preserving a trusted internet, they lack a cohesive center and incentives to move from words to action. Monitoring internet freedom through disparate approaches, promoting tools to avoid censorship, supporting the development of law enforcement capabilities, and creating mechanisms to address cross-border cybercrime have yielded marginal results but do not provide a larger architecture for U.S. policy.

The United States has an opportunity to lead a cohort of nations committed to a shared concept of the internet. Many have argued that the organizing principle of this grouping should be a coalition of democracies that comes together to preserve and extend the value of an open internet.[87] Though the signatories of the 2022 Declaration of the Future of the Internet say they will "work toward an environment that reinforces our democratic systems and promotes active participation of every citizen in democratic processes," the alliance is not explicitly a democratic one. Still in its early stage, the declaration appears too exclusive to form a counterweight to China and Russia, and many important potential partners appear reluctant to join. Most of the signers are in Europe; significant holdouts include Brazil, India, Indonesia, and South Africa.

Making digital trade central to a cyber coalition—instead of a vague definition of democracy or the promotion of unachievable aspiration—would draw more states into the partnership. Being part of a digital trade bloc that includes, for example, the United States, Japan, South Korea, and Europe, could be enough incentive to draw Brazil and India into the fold, particularly if it also includes hardware and outsourced information technology (IT) services. Jointly, the coalition could develop common understanding on the legitimate use of government surveillance, law enforcement access to data, and industrial policies; share best practices on technology regulation; work to forge a trusted supply chain for digital goods and services; and coordinate on international standards.

Joining the coalition does not presuppose an absolute alignment on data privacy or localization policies. Rather, the grouping would build on shared data privacy values while recognizing the differences in domestic approaches to protecting data privacy. Coalition members would be required to develop and implement internet regulations guided by the rule of law, transparency, and accountability. Partners would agree to work cooperatively to address malicious cyber activity and refrain from carrying out malicious acts themselves. As former Japanese Prime Minister Shinzo Abe put it, the goal should be to establish "data flows with trust," not to promote Western-style democracy.[88] A confederated model of internet connectivity and trusted data flow could preserve for its members many of the same values and benefits of the World Wide Web.

Build a digital trade agreement.

The nations that build the next era of digital trade agreements will have a disproportionately significant influence on the future of the world economy. The United States and its partners need to seize this opportunity. The groundwork for this approach has been laid with the USMCA and with the revised KORUS agreement, which together provide a strong model for digital trade chapters and standalone digital trade agreements. In April 2022, the United States, along with Canada, Japan, the Philippines, Singapore, South Korea, and Taiwan, announced the creation of a Global Cross-Border Privacy Rules Forum to promote interoperability and bridge different regulatory approaches to data protection and privacy. The group, which is in principle open to the entry of other countries, will create an international certification system for private businesses transferring data based on privacy protection standards developed by the Asia-Pacific Economic Cooperation.[89] Beyond the United States, Japan, Singapore, and the United Kingdom are leaders in promoting trusted cross-border data flows.

Several agreements can serve as models, including the Economic Partnership Agreement between Japan and the European Union, as well as agreements between Japan and the United Kingdom, Singapore and the United Kingdom, and among Chile, New Zealand, and Singapore.[90] These agreements broadly cover both the removal of tariffs on digital goods and the elimination of nontariff barriers to digital trade. Important shared attributes include

- ensuring the free flow of data across borders;

- prohibiting localization requirements for computing facilities, cloud services, or data analysis motivated by anticompetitive or protectionist purposes; and

- banning requirements to turn over source code, algorithms, or related intellectual property rights.

New or expanded provisions should address concerns of workers and consumers, including those that promote digital inclusiveness, strengthen consumer confidence and trust, and protect personal information.

The United States should lead the effort to build a digital agreement, perhaps using the Digital Economy Partnership Agreement among Chile, New Zealand, and Singapore as a starting point. A regional initiative that includes Australia, Chile, Japan, New Zealand, Singapore, and South Korea, among others, would be a market large enough to influence U.S. firms and a good place to start. It would signal a comprehensive approach rather than a piecemeal, bilateral one. And it would be large enough to draw important states such as India, Indonesia, and Malaysia.[91]

> Agree to and adopt a shared policy on digital privacy that is interoperable with Europe's General Data Protection Regulation.

Sparked by a steady stream of revelations of how technology platforms collect information and a deeper understanding of the dynamics of advertising and the internet economy, consumers around the world are more demanding of regulations that preserve and protect personal data. The United States, the European Union, and like-minded nations should forge a clear consensus on privacy goals.

Efforts to pass comprehensive national domestic privacy legislation have been fitful and spanned more than twenty years. As of May 2022, California, Colorado, Connecticut, Utah, and Virginia have passed state privacy laws. These laws borrow terms, definitions, and procedures from the GDPR, which is increasingly a de facto global standard on the security and incident notification requirements for the storage of personal data. Australia, Brazil, Japan, and South Korea all modeled their privacy legislation on the GDPR.

The GDPR is not perfect, however. Since it took effect in 2018, little action has been taken against Big Tech on their data collection practices. Compliance costs, especially for small businesses, can be burdensome. Endless pop-ups have created "consent fatigue" among users. It has also resulted in unintended restrictions on AI and blockchain use by businesses. Washington can learn from these detriments to make context-specific modifications.

Washington should work with other members of the coalition to develop common privacy principles that are interoperable with the GDPR but require some compromises from Brussels. European policymakers have cloaked their actions in the language of privacy, but recent data localization requirements appear to be motivated by a desire for access to private information by local law enforcement authorities as well as economic protectionism against U.S. technology companies. The United States should offer a quid pro quo: in exchange for formally promoting GDPR-like principles by member states, European states would drop efforts to force data localization or to grant cybersecurity certifications only to European-owned organizations.

Resolve outstanding issues on U.S.-EU data transfers.

Another issue preventing closer coordination between the United States and Europe is access to data by law enforcement or national security agencies. U.S. officials have tried both to reassure Europeans that U.S. intelligence agencies are unlikely to collect data on ordinary citizens and to note that European intelligence and law enforcement agencies' access to private data is often less constrained than that in the United States. The Court of Justice of the European Union has been unconvinced, and in the 2020 Schrems II decision, it invalidated the previously negotiated Privacy Shield agreement on necessary protections for transatlantic data transfers. The CJEU found that the protections offered by the United States were not "essentially equivalent" to those of the GDPR, and individuals in EU territory whose transferred personal data was obtained by U.S. intelligence agencies still did not enjoy "effective legal remedies" before an "independent and impartial court." The CJEU also claimed U.S. surveillance laws lacked proportionality given that bulk collections could not ensure that surveillance occurred only when necessary to meet legitimate security interests.[92] The two sides need to finalize a data transfer agreement.

In March 2022, President Biden and European Commission President Ursula von der Leyen announced that the two sides had reached a new agreement on data flows. Washington would limit disproportionate signals intelligence collection, and European citizens would be able to appeal to an "independent Data Protection Review Court" if they felt their privacy had been violated. The U.S. commitment to the agreement will come through an executive order, which could be reversed by the next administration and is likely to face legal challenges from European privacy groups. The future of transatlantic data flows remains on uncertain legal ground.[93]

As part of this coalition, member countries should agree to a set of practices for providing law enforcement access to the data of their citizens when it is held by another member government and for providing broad, robust, and transparent protections of the data of citizens from coalition partners. These regulations need both be agreed to in treaty form and implemented in national laws. The U.S.-Cloud Act, under which the United States has signed agreements with Australia and the United Kingdom, could be a model for this purpose.[94]

Passing a comprehensive privacy law would significantly respond to the EU's concerns. The United States is already a participant in a discussion at the Organization of Economic Cooperation and Development (OECD) on comparative practices for law enforcement's access to data. While signaling that their preference is a shared understanding with Brussels, U.S. policymakers should remind their European counterparts Washington could take more assertive steps. If the two sides cannot agree on a new regime for data transfer, then the United States could suspend or revoke the measures it already put in place to address EU concerns. The United States could also look to form common cause with Australia, Canada, and the United Kingdom, which also face the threat of inadequacy determination from the European Union.[95]

Create an international cybercrime center.

To both expand digital trade and address malicious cyber activity, future digital trade agreements should require institutions that monitor for violations and coordinate action to punish transgressors. Such agreements should also include binding mechanisms for dispute resolution. Under this approach, standalone institutions could be created to fulfill these functions and then incorporated by reference into any new digital trade chapters or standalone trade agreements. An international crime center could both play this role and promote capacity-building measures among coalition partners.

Operational cooperation between national law enforcement agencies is fragmented and immature, whereas cybercrime is globalized. To improve coordination on cybercrime, the coalition should develop a joint international cybercrime center with a clear focus on crime, not domestic intelligence. Mechanisms exist to coordinate action on law enforcement investigations and information sharing, such as Interpol and the European Cybercrime Centre, but no central, global clearinghouse is in place for requesting law enforcement assistance or supporting coordinated takedown activity for botnets, a network of computers infected with malware and controlled as a group without the owners' knowledge. Currently, coordinated takedown actions require continual resourcing, and a new coalition is formed for each effort.

A new international cybercrime center would serve as a platform for continually pressuring cybercriminals and the infrastructure they use to operate.

In 2014, for example, the Gameover Zeus botnet takedown was made possible by FBI cooperation with law enforcement from Australia, Canada, France, Germany, Italy, Japan, the Netherlands, Ukraine, and others, as well as numerous companies including Dell SecureWorks, CrowdStrike, Microsoft F-Secure, Level 3 Communications, McAfee, Symantec, Sophos, and Trend Micro. The 2021 takedown of the Emotet botnet involved similar partnerships.[96] The operational effectiveness of these past ad hoc efforts needs to be institutionalized and routinized, and existing efforts coordinated by the National Cyber Forensics Training Alliance as well as bilateral efforts like the recently announced U.S.-Israeli task force on ransomware should be shifted to this center.[97]

A new international cybercrime center would serve as a platform for continually pressuring cybercriminals and undermining the infrastructure they use to operate, including tracking and reclaiming cryptocurrency that funds criminal activity. It would be closely tied to financial regulators and host law enforcement agencies, civilian computer emergency response teams, internet service providers, cloud platforms, nongovernmental organizations, academia, and cybersecurity firms. Each member would be expected to provide support to the center, including analysis and planning capabilities. Nonmember states would be invited to provide a liaison to the center to coordinate law enforcement and takedown activities within their jurisdiction. The center should publicly have ties to offensive cyber units within member states to coordinate offensive action against criminal platforms when voluntary action, law enforcement, and diplomacy fail.

Create a focused program for cyber aid and infrastructure development.

A growing part of China's ambitious Belt and Road Initiative (BRI) is focused on digital infrastructure. Beijing has identified 5G technology, smart cities, utilization of the Beidou satellite system, communication infrastructure, network connectivity, and telecommunications services as central areas of focus. It often offers BRI countries complete technology packages, including cloud services, mobile payments, smart cities, and social media applications from a combination of Chinese companies.[98] The United States and its partners also need to address global demands for technology infrastructure.

During the Trump administration, U.S. officials warned of the cybersecurity risks of relying on Chinese tech infrastructure, stressing the potential threats of data collection and disruption. Washington was less successful in providing alternatives to countries attracted by the cheaper prices and reliability of Chinese technology or developing a cybersecurity roadmap for those likely to adopt a mix of U.S. and Chinese hardware, software, and services. The United States and its coalition partners need to create funding mechanisms for the development of digital infrastructure. Congress should consolidate the State Department's foreign assistance funding and add a new line for cyber capacity building in the State, Foreign Operations, and Related Programs appropriations legislation.[99] This effort, however, needs to do more than provide an alternative source of funding. Business, government, and civil society groups should also partner to demonstrate how these technologies can be deployed to protect privacy and individual liberties.

The coalition should be a competitor in the race to link the remaining 2.9 billion people without connectivity to the global internet. Special emphasis should be placed on the continued expansion of undersea cables, which can both blunt growing Chinese investments in this infrastructure and provide a more diverse network with fewer single points of failure for global internet communications.

Planned investments by the United States, Australia, and Japan to connect a series of Pacific islands are a model of the actions the coalition should take.[100] Australia has also invested in cables to connect to other island nations in the Indian Ocean. These investments, however, pale in comparison to those made by private-sector actors, notably Google, which has committed $1 billion to an undersea cable to connect several African nations to Europe.[101] Private companies should take the lead in these initiatives, with the coalition providing support only when investments do not make financial sense to the private sector.

The coalition and its private-sector partners should build, along with infrastructure projects, the capacity to counter malicious cyber activity. Efforts should not only target traditional areas of technical assistance, such as the development of laws to govern digital activity and law enforcement capability, but also build military and intelligence capabilities among allied states. These should include defensive and attribution tools, but potentially also offensive tools to act as a deterrent and raise the cost of interference for adversary states.

Build a coalition for open-source software.

Open-source software (i.e., software that is free and open to anyone to inspect and modify) is widely used and deployed in commercial as well as critical infrastructure and national security networks. Outside of major curated and supported projects, the code is often maintained by a small group of volunteers, with ad hoc, under-resourced efforts to sustain software security. Coalition partners should work together to develop and maintain open-source code, as well as ensure its security.

In December 2021, a Chinese security researcher notified the Apache Software Foundation of a vulnerability in Log4J, widely used code that records and communicates diagnostic messages to system administrators and users. Log4J is almost everywhere in the software ecosystem. Jen Easterly, director of the Cybersecurity and Infrastructure Security Agency, called the vulnerability the most serious she had seen in her career.[102] A large number of hackers scanned the internet to exploit the flaw, and the cybersecurity firm Mandiant found APT41, a group associated with the MSS, using Log4J to target U.S. state governments.[103]

In response to Log4J, the White House quickly convened a group to discuss how to prevent security defects in open-source codes, improve the process for finding defects and fixing them, and shorten the response time for distributing and implementing solutions.[104] Open-source software is not inherently less secure than proprietary software. In fact, well-supported open-source products could be even more secure than their proprietary counterparts, given the participation of large communities of developers. *Well-supported* is the crucial factor. Two important elements of well-supported open-source products are incentives, such as bug bounties, for developers to find flaws and investment by the affected companies to accelerate the remediation of those flaws.

The United States and its international partners should promote the adoption and promulgation of open standards among users, particularly by major technology providers. They should also work together to make the open standards process international, transparent, and fully aligned with cybersecurity objectives. The Linux Foundation, Cloud Native Compute Foundation, and Open Titan are all examples of standards bodies with transparent and consensus-driven processes. In addition, the coalition partners should support improvements in security of open-source software through consortia such as the Open Source Security Foundation, a cross-industry collaboration that is developing security tools, best practices, and a software ecosystem for vulnerability disclosures.

Work jointly across partners to retain technology superiority.

Technology advantages that accrue over several years can ultimately prove evanescent. The United States and its allies need to increase investment in research in sectors that will be critical to cyber competition in the coming decade. Semiconductors, AI, quantum information, and data sciences are fields in which the United States cannot afford to fall behind. Congress should pass the Innovation and Competition Act/America Competes Act, which would increase investment in science and technology, provide $50 billion for semiconductor research and manufacturing, and invest in U.S. leadership in international standards organizations.

It will not be enough to remain ahead in basic research. The United States and its allies will also need to lead in the identification, application, and evaluation of artificial intelligence and quantum computing to cyber and other national security challenges. As the final National Security Commission on Artificial Intelligence report recommends, the United States needs to establish trusted sources of materials and components for quantum computers, invest in the development of hybrid quantum-classical algorithms, and focus on the fielding of national security applications. Washington should also incentivize the private sector to invest in national security applications by announcing specific government-use cases of quantum computers.[105]

Although most of the media attention paid to AUKUS, the trilateral security agreement among Australia, the United Kingdom, and the United States announced in September 2021, was on sharing nuclear submarine technology, the group will also focus on cyber capabilities, quantum technologies, and artificial intelligence.[106] The Pentagon should also coordinate with its Australian and British counterparts on developing shared test, evaluation, validation, and verification infrastructure for artificial intelligence.

The United States should announce a cybersecurity "grand challenge" for universities and private companies in its Quad partners (Australia, India, and Japan). In 2016, a powerful machine called Mayhem designed by a Pittsburgh company won the Cyber Grand Challenge, a cybersecurity competition held by the U.S. Defense Advanced Research Projects Agency. Mayhem won by automatically detecting, patching, and exploiting software security vulnerabilities, and the Pentagon now uses the technology in all military branches. The Quad announced in September 2021 initiatives to drive the adoption and implementation of shared cyber standards, develop secure software, and grow the tech workforce, but the group should also catalyze technological breakthroughs.

In addition, Washington should build on its bilateral science and technology relationships. In April 2021, President Biden and former Japanese Prime Minister Yoshihide Suga launched the Competitiveness and Resilience Partnership and committed $4.5 billion to R&D on 5G, quantum computing, and artificial intelligence. Washington should similarly deepen funding pools on shared strategic priorities with Brussels, Canberra, London, and Seoul.

Balance Targeted Pressure, Disruptive Cyber Operations, and Pragmatic Norms

Norms are difficult to perpetuate and easily abandoned. Nonetheless, as this American-driven coalition develops, Washington and its partners should declare a set of norms that they will allow to constrain their cyber operations. The United States should also discuss a set of understandings with potential adversaries, China and Russia in particular. These restraints are motivated in part by self-interest, as they could help prevent unintended and catastrophic outcomes. U.S. policymakers should, however, make clear that this self-restraint will guide U.S. operations above the threshold for the use of force or armed attack, and that for operations below the threshold, the United States will continue to adopt a more proactive, initiative-seizing posture.

> The United States should declare norms against destructive attacks on election and financial systems.

After consultation with allies and friends, Washington should announce an initial set of standards for self-restraint in cyberspace. Along with repeating commitments to abide by international law—including international humanitarian law and the laws of armed conflict—officials should state that the United States will refrain from destructive attacks on election infrastructure and the international financial system.

Across the world, more countries are relying on digital infrastructure to manage elections. During the 2016 election, according to U.S. intelligence reports, the Russian government directed cyber activity targeted at state election infrastructure, though there was no evidence that any votes were changed. Scanning election infrastructure was the most widespread activity, and Russian hackers successfully gained access to and removed data from infrastructure in two states. Russian operators also conducted operations against a widely used vendor of election systems. In January 2017, the U.S. Department of Homeland Security designated election systems as critical infrastructure, bringing them under the protection of the federal government.[107]

The United States and its partners should promote a norm regarding disruptive attacks against election infrastructure, banning efforts to disrupt voter registration, voting machines, vote counting, and election announcements. It should work with coalition partners to prevent, mitigate, and, when necessary, respond to destructive attacks on election infrastructure.

The global financial system is highly interconnected and depends on trust. Cyber operations directed at the integrity of any one part of the system could cascade into others, threatening the entire system and international stability. Washington should declare that it will not conduct operations against the integrity of the data of financial institutions and the availability of critical financial systems.[108]

Given that norms exert a weak limit on state actions in cyberspace, the United States and its partners should be prepared for their violation by increasing the resilience and redundancy of these critical systems. Financial institutions should regularly run exercises to restore the integrity of data after a cyberattack. The declaration of these norms, however, signals that these types of attacks will be considered off limits and mobilize coalition partners quickly to respond if the norm is violated.

> Negotiate with adversaries to establish limits on cyber operations directed at nuclear command, control, and communication systems.

Although bilateral and multilateral discussion on norms have so far been of limited use, the United States has a strong shared interest in working with potential adversaries to prevent cyberattacks from worsening or creating a nuclear crisis.

During a conventional conflict, states could be tempted to use cyberattacks to try to neutralize nuclear threats. These actions, however, would be highly destabilizing. Cyberattacks on NC3 systems could lead to incentives for states to launch nuclear weapons preemptively if they feared that they could lose their second-strike capability. Intelligence gathering could be interpreted by the defender as efforts to degrade nuclear capabilities. Cyberattacks on nuclear systems could produce false warnings or miscalculations, interfere with communications or access to information vital to decisions about the use of nuclear weapons, and increase the risk of unauthorized use of a weapon.[109] Cyberattacks on space assets involved in command and control would be equally destabilizing because of their close connections to assured second-strike capabilities.

These risks are rising as modern NC3 systems come to depend more heavily on digital infrastructure. In a 2020 report, the Nuclear Threat Initiative found that "almost 9 out of 10 planned nuclear modernization programs involve at least some new digital components or upgrades."[110]

The United States should enter into discussions with China and Russia about limiting all types of cyber operations against NC3 systems on land and in space. In addition, participants in these discussions should commit to separating conventional from nuclear command and control systems as much as possible. Given that a cyber intrusion designed for espionage could look identical to an offensive operation, all sides have a strong interest in prohibiting all types of operations to prevent miscalculation that could lead to a nuclear strike.

In the wake of the Russian invasion of Ukraine and the growing geopolitical competition between the United States and China, the spaces for cooperation between Washington and Moscow and Washington and Beijing are extremely narrow. Declarations of self-restraint can function as confidence-building measures, perhaps bridging the trust gap. However, previous instances of cooperation in cyberspace—the 2015 U.S.-China cyber espionage agreement or the joint Russian-U.S. investigations of online credit card theft in the mid-1990s—coincided with more amicable periods in the larger bilateral relationship.[111] U.S. policymakers should make clear that they are entering discussions with their Chinese and Russian counterparts because understandings on cyber operations and nuclear command and control are a shared interest among the three powers in preventing catastrophic outcomes.

U.S. policymakers should also be prepared to fail in bilateral negotiations and to continue unilateral measures of risk reduction. These include making NC3 structures less subject to incidental cyberattacks and more resilient if they are attacked, as well as preparing NC3 systems for information warfare and the authentication of good information. Policymakers will also need to ensure that the internal processes to decide whether to proceed with a potentially escalatory cyber operation are robust enough to clearly weigh the strategic risks against the intelligence and military benefits.[112]

Develop coalition-wide practices for the Vulnerabilities Equities Process.

When the U.S. intelligence community, law enforcement agencies, or other government actors discover a zero-day vulnerability, they face a decision of whether to disclose the vulnerability to the private sector or keep the vulnerability secret to facilitate future offensive capabilities. In addition, zero days can be bought and sold in certain markets, some legal, others underground.[113] Disclosing to industry can result in timely patching and bolster national and personal security. Retaining and using the vulnerabilities can benefit national security through intelligence gathering and disrupted adversary operations.

The NSA, for example, reportedly developed a hacking tool known as EternalBlue that exploited a vulnerability in Microsoft. Even though some U.S. officials allegedly wanted to reveal the vulnerability to the company, the NSA used the tool for more than five years.[114] The tool, however, was eventually stolen and repackaged by cybercriminals to become the basis of WannaCry, the North Korean ransomware attack that spread across the globe, and NotPetya, a Russian cyberattack against Ukraine that boomeranged around the world, hitting conglomerates such as Maersk, Merck, Mondelez, and Pfizer, and became the most costly cyberattack to date. Washington has led in the development of the process to evaluate when to share vulnerabilities with the private sector, and it should help expand the process to its coalition partners.

A 2008 presidential directive established what became the Vulnerabilities Equities Process, an interagency procedure the U.S. government uses to decide whether to disclose vulnerabilities or hold them for potential offensive operations. A U.S. official stated that the government's bias is toward disclosure and explained that the process attempts to determine the extent to which the vulnerability is in use, how useful it is, how likely it is to be discovered, how damaging it would be in adversarial hands, whether another government has access to it, and whether it can be patched.[115]

The VEP periodically revisits undisclosed zero-day vulnerabilities to assess whether conditions have shifted toward disclosure. Over the last few years, the NSA has steadily increased the number of public disclosures and advisories. This should be further supported and will require additional funding.

The VEP stands in sharp contrast to recent developments in China. Beijing banned Chinese security researchers from attending international hacking events and competitions (which they regularly won), and new regulations require all software security vulnerabilities to be reported to the government first. These regulations appear to have significantly improved Chinese offensive capabilities as Chinese government hackers have moved from simpler methods to more powerful zero-day vulnerabilities. Aggressive Chinese assaults on American computer networks in 2021, for example, used zero-day vulnerabilities in Microsoft Exchange systems and Pulse Security VPNs. A Chinese researcher at Alibaba did report the Log4J vulnerability to Apache, but the Ministry of Industry and Information Technology suspended cooperation with Alibaba Cloud for six months for not reporting in China first.[116]

As its adversaries rely more heavily on zero-day attacks, the United States should reprioritize cyber defense and encourage partners to develop similar processes.[117] As a result of American leadership, Australia, Canada, and the United Kingdom released publicly their equities processes. The Netherlands announced that it has put a VEP in place but has not released any details on the process.[118] The three countries should work together to help other coalition partners implement VEPs. In the past, intelligence agencies have not taken credit for zero-day disclosures to software makers. They stand to gain greater credibility with the private sector by claiming credit for these public disclosures. The United States and its allies should also conduct national awareness campaigns around the urgency of patching, given that critical systems still remain unpatched months—even years—after a patch becomes available.

Adopt greater transparency about defend forward actions.

U.S. and partner statements about self-restraint around a set of targets should be part of a more proactive strategy to disrupt and mitigate adversarial cyber operations below the level of armed conflict. This strategy includes Cyber Command's persistent engagement as well as diplomatic, economic, and intelligence operations aiming to seize the initiative in cyberspace. In effect, the United States should develop a broad effort to erode adversarial capabilities, making them less effective by taking out infrastructure; exposing tools; and creating political, diplomatic, and economic pressure on finances, authorities, and leadership.

Proactive measures can take different forms. In October 2020, Cyber Command hacked the command and control servers to cut off TrickBot, the world's largest criminal botnet, briefly slowing its operations. This activity was followed by efforts to disrupt TrickBot by private companies including Microsoft, ESET, Symantec, and Lumen Technologies.[119]

U.S. policymakers should consider not only deploying cyber capabilities in advance of, and even during, future conflicts but also messaging clearly and publicly that those forces are active. One of the reasons cyber operations appear not to have influenced the beginning stages of the Russia-Ukraine war could be the preemptive deployment of CYBERCOM mission forces and EU cyber rapid response team experts to Ukraine to "hunt forward," or to look for active cyber threats on critical infrastructure networks.[120]

Washington's strategy of proactive transparency and information sharing in the early days of the Russia-Ukraine war, even with tightly held intelligence, is another successful example of seizing the initiative. In the days before the invasion, Washington provided specific information about possible false flag operations, troop positions, and coup attempts. These efforts not only gave the United States first-mover advantages in the information space but also forced Russia to react to and consider its own intelligence weaknesses.[121]

Hold states accountable for malicious activity emanating from their territory.

The power of nonstate actors seeking to antagonize the U.S. government and private sector has grown dramatically in recent decades. Much as states across the globe cracked down on foreign safe havens for terrorists, yet recognizing some important differences, the United States and its partners should take a tough stance against states that deliberately provide cybercriminal safe havens.

Many states agree that turning a blind eye to highly damaging cybercriminal activity emanating from its territory would breach an international legal duty, such that proportionate countermeasures could be allowable.[122] To address the problem of states that actively harbor cybercriminals or ignore third parties using their digital infrastructure in offensive and criminal campaigns, the United States and its coalition partners could set a policy similar to the response to international terrorism that they will hold accountable any states that provide safe havens or do not cooperate in the takedown of criminal infrastructure or in law enforcement investigations, arrests, and extradition. Washington should exert diplomatic and economic pressure, but under certain circumstances could also reserve the right to take action against infrastructure used by these groups if the countries hosting it will not do so.

Get the U.S. House in Order

The third pillar of a realistic cyber policy is focused on actions the United States should take at home. As noted earlier, a range of domestic policies would improve U.S. cyber defenses, such as reporting laws and information sharing that are beyond the scope of this Task Force. However, given the integral relationship of these measures to U.S. foreign policy, the report highlights the need to make digital competition part of national security strategy, to clean up the U.S. internet, to address the intelligence gap, and to bolster cyber and technical talent.

> Make digital competition a pillar of the national security strategy.

The last three published White House national security strategies have addressed cybersecurity matters. The Biden administration's forthcoming recommendations should go further by recognizing that cyberspace is now one of the indisputably central domains in which the United States competes with its adversaries. This competition is taking place on multiple levels: intelligence collection, disinformation, criminal activity, military action, and, most important, economics.

The national security strategy should include digital competition as one of its main pillars. It should acknowledge that the leverage the United States has to punish bad actors will often lie outside the cyber domain. Cybersecurity challenges, offensive and defensive, will never be addressed solely in the digital realm; they will require nontechnical, political, diplomatic, military, and economic measures.[123] Any successful cyber strategy will therefore necessarily mirror a successful foreign policy. The United States should build coalitions and lead by example as it attempts to reinforce a rules-based international order. It should develop the tools and capabilities needed for dealing with inevitable failures and setback. In effect, the National Security Council should coordinate a cross-domain, mutually reinforcing strategy that disrupts, discloses, and contests malicious cyberspace behavior. On the other side of the ledger, cyber capabilities should be added to the list of tools the United States can bring to bear in the international arena. Cyber should be part of the diplomatic, intelligence, military, and economic paradigm.

The national security strategy would prompt subordinate strategy documents on how the U.S. government will address various aspects of cybersecurity. These documents, however, are no substitute for making cyber central to the national security strategy. The importance of the national security strategy for setting budget and agency priorities cannot be overstated.

Clean up U.S. cyberspace by offering incentives for ISPs and cloud providers to reduce malicious activity within their infrastructure.

A doctrine of holding other states accountable could invite other countries to target U.S. infrastructure. In most offensive campaigns, the intermediate infrastructure is often U.S. infrastructure that has either been compromised or purchased. At present, U.S. internet service providers are considered common carriers that are simply passing along bits regardless of whether their network traffic is malicious. ISPs have few incentives to clean up traffic and face significant risks if they choose to do so. Similarly, cloud providers today are routinely used to stage attacks and are treated as intermediate victims to the ultimate crime. They lack incentives and liability structures to reduce the weaponization of their technology. ISPs and cloud providers should be incentivized and encouraged to identify and reduce malicious activities occurring on or through their infrastructure.

Despite examples of the FBI deleting malware from infected U.S. systems, such as a recent effort to remove malware developed by China's Ministry of State Security, this capability is not regularly used.[124] Additional updates to the Federal Rules of Criminal Procedures would allow for stronger, faster mechanisms for notice and takedown of malicious activity. The United States should improve its ability to detect malicious foreign activity overseas and increase the speed with which that information is shared with targeted companies and federal law enforcement. Further, Washington should strengthen "know your customer" requirements.

Address the domestic intelligence gap.

This report focuses on American global interests in cyberspace, but a comprehensive U.S. government response to alleviate the threat from a multitude of actors has a domestic component as well. The NSA has the capability to detect many threats from overseas, but adversaries' using U.S. infrastructure creates a blind spot in U.S. defenses. Adversaries take advantage of the slow and bureaucratic processes for handing off NSA intelligence for follow-up by the FBI and other federal law enforcement agencies. The Department of Justice and Congress should work together to reform the process for seeking warrants to allow for "hot pursuit" in cyberspace.

These reforms are necessary, but U.S. policy should be unequivocal that the government is not seeking the authority for the NSA or any other agency to have broad surveillance powers on the domestic internet. The U.S. government should not take over the protection of private-sector enterprise networks. Strengthening voluntary information sharing and incident reporting is likely the best approach to addressing the domestic intelligence gap.

Promote the exchange of and collaboration among talent from trusted partners.

The United States and its partners face a severe shortage of cyber and technical expertise. According to the National Institute of Standards and Technology, the global shortage of cybersecurity professionals is estimated to be 2.72 million.[125] Washington has much to do at home to address the talent gap, including new programs to attract and retain talent in the public sector with competitive salaries, efforts to recruit from minority-serving institutions and military associations, the revision of immigration rules, and the promotion of a welcoming environment for foreign students and researchers in the United States. Nevertheless, Washington should also use talent exchanges and development programs to draw coalition partners more closely together. The United States will need to invest in the next generation of people-to-people connections.

As part of its Indo-Pacific strategy, for example, the Biden administration announced a new Quad fellowship program that will support graduate studies of American, Australian, Indian, and Japanese students in STEM (science, technology, engineering, and mathematics) fields.[126] A new Quad cybersecurity fellowship, funded by the participating governments and the private sector, will not only bring fellows together twice a year to address "wicked problems" in information security, but also place fellows in short-term postings in the public or private sector outside of their home countries.

Washington should also facilitate talent exchanges and research collaboration among a larger number of trusted partners by convening workshops among information security researchers, fostering networks of cybersecurity experts, and coordinating with the private sector on cybersecurity workforce training. A U.S. Cybersecurity Training Institute, modeled on the U.S. Telecommunication Training Institute, could bring officials from developing countries to the United States for tuition-free training in cybersecurity technologies and best practices.

Develop expertise for cyber foreign policy.

Over the last five years, the military and intelligence agencies have often, with understandable reason, taken leadership roles in cyberspace. Washington needs now to strengthen its diplomatic influence in cyberspace. The United States was initially the leader in cyber diplomacy, establishing the office of the cyber coordinator in 2011. Other countries quickly followed suit, institutionalizing and expanding the role, while the cyber coordinator office was eliminated in a 2017 State Department reorganization. The idea for a new office in the State Department had bipartisan support on the Hill but did not come to fruition until April 2022, when Secretary of State Antony Blinken announced the creation of the Bureau of Cyberspace and Digital Policy.[127]

Establishing a State Department cyber bureau as well as appointing a cyber ambassador and special envoy for emerging technology are important first steps in placing State back in the lead in tech diplomacy, strengthening the department in the interagency process, and ensuring that the United States has the technical competencies needed to supplement the traditional methods and processes of diplomacy and trade. The Biden administration is reportedly considering allowing the State Department greater ability to monitor and weigh in on third-party notifications, decisions on when and how the U.S. government notifies others if the United States plans to enter their cyberspace to disrupt adversaries.[128] Such a move would clearly strengthen the bureau's role in the interagency process as well as in its interaction with diplomatic partners.

Within the State Department, familiarity and experience with digital and cyber issues should be considered central to career development. Just as joint-service education and experience are now required for promotion in the military, all Foreign Service officers, not just those in the cyber bureau, should spend time working on digital and cyber topics. Career Foreign Service officers up for an ambassadorial appointment should have done a tour in one of several tech roles at the department or across the U.S. government. The State Department should work with the private sector and academia to develop training programs for government officials to build expertise and understanding in cyber-related topics. The department should also look to personnel loans from tech firms or academic institutions who can join a cyber diplomacy team for a short period and support its mission.

Cyber diplomacy requires a government-wide approach. The government, business, and academia, therefore, need to do more to build expertise on cyber-related issues across the public and private sectors. Higher education institutions should provide cybersecurity students with more real-world experience through internships, capstones, and co-ops. Universities should require computer science majors to take at least one class in cybersecurity and broaden cybersecurity programs beyond one department, facilitating inclusion from multiple departments. This would expose cybersecurity students to domain-specific knowledge required in the workplace and business, law, engineering, and political science students to how cybersecurity is relevant to their fields.

In addition, colleges and universities, as well as high schools, should add introductory computer science as a requirement for graduation. Some states already are making this change for high schools. The objective is to spur interest and basic understanding in the technological language that is reshaping the world and to expand the talent pool. In 2020, the Senate had just three engineers. The policymakers of tomorrow cannot make good cyber policy if they have no understanding of the basics of computer science. Business, academia, and the government should also cooperate to create and fund a White House fellowship for tech talent. Each cohort would tie business and the tech sector closer together as the fellows move along their careers.[129]

CONCLUSION

A modified U.S. cyber strategy will be more limited, more realistic, and more likely to succeed in achieving critical but finite goals. It would not seek for other countries to embrace an American definition of democracy or free speech, but rather secure a commitment to build the domestic capacities to ensure the trusted flow of data. Although a modified strategy assumes that the United States will more proactively use cyber and non-cyber tools to disrupt cyberattacks and that norms are more useful in binding friends and allies together than in constraining adversaries, the strategy also takes into account that the major cyber powers share some interests in preventing certain types of destructive and disruptive attacks.

A modified U.S. strategy needs to overcome two major challenges.

First is the failure to bridge the cybersecurity and commercial divide with Europe. Policymakers in Washington and Brussels increasingly see the need for a strong transatlantic partnership in response to Beijing's and Moscow's assertiveness in cyberspace. The drive for technological autonomy and data localization in Europe, however, could make it difficult to convert a shared perception of the rising threat of cyberspace into expeditious action. A more realistic cyber policy would allow the United States more flexibility. If it fails to make progress with Europe, Washington could pivot to other digital powers such as India, Japan, Singapore, and South Korea in pursuit of the same policy goals.

Second is domestic inaction. The United States needs to move quickly on many issues, particularly domestic privacy legislation and developing cyber expertise for foreign policy practitioners. Most important, policymakers need to recognize the urgency of cyber and digital action. Failing to act now will significantly threaten U.S. security and economic interests in the future.

The policies of the last thirty years were rooted in American history and values. But that approach failed to prevent the internet from becoming a more fragmented and dangerous ecosystem. It is increasingly difficult for the United States to maneuver, while adversaries develop and implement comprehensive strategies for projecting power through, and exerting influence over, cyberspace. It is time for a more realistic U.S. cyber policy that consolidates a coalition of allies and friends around the principle of the trusted and secure flow of data, matches more assertive efforts to disrupt cyber operations with clear statements about self-imposed restraint, and prioritizes digital competition in national security strategies.

ADDITIONAL VIEWS

History shows that societies take time to learn how to respond to major disruptive technological change and to develop norms that stabilize expectations. It took two to three decades after the bombing of Hiroshima to develop agreements regarding nuclear weapons. Norms to govern the risks posed by cyber technology are likely to evolve slowly, not based on good will but from states' self-interest in coordination, reputation, and prudence. Even at the height of the Cold War, the United States and its adversaries worked together to develop rules of the road based on such self-interest. Our report offers some useful recommendations about norms, but we could go further. For instance, the Global Commission on Stability in Cyberspace has suggested a norm to protect the core infrastructure of the internet from attack. The "open global internet" may be over, but self-interest in coordination and communication remains, even among adversaries.

—Joseph S. Nye Jr.
joined by Guillermo S. Christensen and Amy B. Zegart

I wish to qualify the finding that cybercrime is a national security threat. This is not meant to compare confronting cybercrime to the war on drugs of the late twentieth century, which viewed the global criminal narcotics trade as a national security threat. To be sure, the vast majority of current cybercrime, and many of the examples we cite in the report, do not yet truly represent a threat to the territorial or political integrity of the United States (an obvious exception being Russian interference in U.S. elections).

However, unlike the narcotics trade that provoked the war on drugs, it is the combination of cybercrime trends and the evolution of their enabling environment—a fragmented, less free, more dangerous internet—that drives the threat to such a level. A fragmented internet means adversarial governments can more easily refuse to cooperate with global standards and norms; trust will continue to be a precious commodity that is easy to degrade, difficult to defend, and even more difficult to restore; and the current, robust state-enabled industry of "CrimTech" or crime-as-a-service will escalate to conflict-as-a-service.

These qualities amount to a manifest threat to national security. An appropriate comparison is the evolution of international terrorism—and its enabling environment—from a largely criminal matter to a national security threat that eventually precipitated two decades of armed conflict; this comparison is reflected in our recommendation to hold states accountable for malicious activity in their borders.

—Neal A. Pollard
joined by Guillermo S. Christensen

ENDNOTES

1. Adam Satariano and Valerie Hopkins, "Russia, Blocked From the Global Internet, Plunges Into Digital Isolation," *New York Times*, March 7, 2022, https://www.nytimes.com/2022/03/07/technology/russia-ukraine-internet-isolation.html; Joseph Menn, Ellen Nakashima, and Craig Timberg, "Lumen, a Second Major American Internet Carrier, Pulling Out of Russia," *Washington Post*, March 8, 2022, https://www.washingtonpost.com/technology/2022/03/08/lumen-internet-russia-backbone-cut.

2. Adrian Shahbaz and Allie Funk, "Freedom on the Net 2021: The Global Drive to Control Big Tech," Freedom House, September 21, 2021, https://freedomhouse.org/report/freedom-net/2021/global-drive-control-big-tech.

3. Gian M. Volpicelli, "The Draconian Rise of Internet Shutdowns," *Wired*, February 9, 2021, https://www.wired.co.uk/article/internet-shutdowns; Access Now, *The Return of Digital Authoritarianism: Internet Shutdowns in 2021*, April 2022, https://www.accessnow.org/cms/assets/uploads/2022/04/2021-KeepItOn-Report-1.pdf.

4. BBC, "Ukraine Power Cut Was Cyber-Attack," January 11, 2017, https://www.bbc.com/news/technology-38573074; Andy Greenberg, "The Untold Story of NotPetya, the Most Devastating Cyberattack in History," *Wired*, August 22, 2018, https://www.wired.com/story/notpetya-cyberattack-ukraine-russia-code-crashed-the-world.

5. Kate Conger, "Ukraine Says It Thwarted a Sophisticated Russian Cyberattack on Its Power Grid," *New York Times*, April 12, 2022, https://www.nytimes.com/2022/04/12/us/politics/ukraine-russian-cyberattack.html; James Pearson, Raphael Satter, Christopher Bing, and Joel Schectman, "U.S. Spy Agency Probes Sabotage of Satellite Internet During Russian Invasion, Sources Say," Reuters, March 11, 2022, https://www.reuters.com/world/europe/exclusive-us-spy-agency-probes-sabotage-satellite-internet-during-russian-2022-03-11/; CISA, FBI, Joint Cyber Adversary, "Destructive Malware Targeting Organizations in Ukraine," CISA, March 1, 2022, https://www.cisa.gov/uscert/ncas/alerts/aa22-057a; Gordon Corera, "Russia Hacked Ukrainian Satellite Communications, Officials Believe," BBC, March 25, 2022, https://www.bbc.com/news/technology-60796079.

6. Tom Burt, "The Hybrid War in Ukraine," *Microsoft on the Issues* (blog), April 27, 2022, https://blogs.microsoft.com/on-the-issues/2022/04/27/hybrid-war-ukraine-russia-cyberattacks.

7. Alex Scroxton, "Conti Ransomware Syndicate Behind Attack on Irish Health Service," *Computer Weekly*, May 17, 2021, https://www.computerweekly.com/news/252500905/Conti-ransomware-syndicate-behind-attack-on-Irish-health-service; Congressional Research Services, *Colonial Pipeline: The DarkSide Strikes*, May 11, 2021, https://crsreports.congress.gov/product/pdf/IN/IN11667; Jacob Bunge, "JBS Paid 11 Million to Resolve Ransomware Attack," *Wall Street Journal*, June 9, 2021, https://www.wsj.com/articles/jbs-paid-11-million-to-resolve-ransomware-attack-11623280781?mod=hp_lead_pos2; "Cyber Insurance Market Overview: Fourth Quarter 2021," Marsh McLennan, 2021, https://www.marsh.com/us/services/cyber-risk/insights/cyber-insurance-market-overview-q4-2021.html.

8. IT Army of Ukraine (@ITarmyUA), "Hackers all around the world: target #Belarus in the name of #Anonymous," Twitter, February 28, 2022, https://twitter.com/ITarmyUA/status/1498287273581944843?s=20&t=fybBWPvIlxlNEnCm7ZD2ZA; Cyberknow, "2022 Russia-Ukraine War—Cyber Group Tracker," Medium, February 27, 2022, https://cyberknow.medium.com/2022-russia-ukraine-war-cyber-group-tracker-6e08ef31c533.

9. Bill Marczak, John Scott-Railton, Sarah McKune, Bahr Abdul Razzak, and Ron Deibert, *Hide and Seek: Tracking NSO Group's Pegasus Spyware to Operations in 45 Countries*, Citizens Lab, September 18, 2018, https://citizenlab.ca/2018/09/hide-and-seek-tracking-nso-groups-pegasus-spyware-to-operations-in-45-countries; Washington Post Staff, "Takeaways From the Pegasus Project," *Washington Post*, August 2, 2021, https://www.washingtonpost.com/investigations/2021/07/18/takeaways-nso-pegasus-project.

10. U.S. Cyberspace Solarium Commission, *A Warning From Tomorrow: Final Report*, March 11, 2020, https://www.solarium.gov.

11. Martin Matishak, "Biden Signs Cyber Incident Reporting Bill Into Law," *The Record*, March 15, 2022, https://therecord.media/biden-signs-cyber-incident-reporting-bill-into-law.

12. Richard Lei, "Al Gore Takes a Spin on the Info Highway," *Washington Post*, January 14, 1994, https://www.washingtonpost.com/archive/lifestyle/1994/01/14/al-gore-takes-a-spin-on-the-info-highway/2fa7774b-0cb4-45e2-87dc-dfe254001093; Michael L. Best and Keegan W. Wade, "The Internet and Democracy: Global Catalyst or Democratic Dud?" *Bulletin of Science, Technology, and Society* 29, no. 4 (2009): 255–56, doi: 10.1177/0270467609336304.

13. James A. Lewis, "Sovereignty and the Evolution of Internet Ideology," Center for Strategic and International Studies, October 30, 2020, https://www.csis.org/analysis/sovereignty-and-evolution-internet-ideology; "Highlights of Clinton Speech on Internet Freedom," Reuters, January 21, 2010, https://www.reuters.com/article/us-google-china-clinton-highlights/highlights-of-clinton-speech-on-internet-freedom-idUSTRE60K4R820100121.

14. European Union Parliament and Council of the European Union, "General Data Protection Regulation," April 27, 2016, https://eur-lex.europa.eu/legal-content/EN/TXT/PDF/?uri=CELEX:32016R0679; EY Americas, "How To Prepare for Global Data Compliance," EY, May 4, 2021, https://www.ey.com/en_us/consulting/how-to-prepare-for-global-data-compliance; Madalina Murariu, *Data Sharing Between the United States and European Union: Impact of the Schrems II Decision*, Belfer Center, July 2021, https://www.belfercenter.org/publication/data-sharing-between-united-states-and-european-union.

15. Foo Yun Chee, "EU Plans 'Chip Act' To Promote Semiconductor Self-Sufficiency," Reuters, September 15, 2021, https://www.reuters.com/world/europe/tech-is-make-or-break-issue-eu-chief-executive-says-2021-09-15/.

16. "Versailles Declaration: Strengthening European Sovereignty and Reducing Strategic Dependencies," March 11, 2022, https://www.consilium.europa.eu/media/54773/20220311-versailles-declaration-en.pdf.

17. Graham Webster, "A Brief History of the Chinese Internet," *Logic*, May 1, 2019, https://logicmag.io/china/a-brief-history-of-the-chinese-internet; Qijia Zhou, "Building the (Fire) Wall: Internet Censorship in the United States and China," *Harvard International Review*, December 28, 2020, https://hir.harvard.edu/building-the-fire-wall; Gary King, Jennifer Pan, and Margaret E. Roberts, "How Censorship in China Allows Government Criticism but Silences Collective Expression," *American Political Science Review*, 107, no. 2 (2013): 1–18, https://j.mp/2nxNUhk.

18. Andrei Soldatov and Irina Borogan, *The Red Web: The Struggle Between Russia's Digital Dictators and the New Online Revolutionaries* (New York: PublicAffairs, 2015); Nick Macfie and Alexander Marrow, "Russia Disconnects From Internet in Tests as It Bolsters Security," Reuters, July 22, 2021, https://www.reuters.com/technology/russia-disconnected-global-internet-tests-rbc-daily-2021-07-22; Merrit Kennedy, "Russia's 'Sovereign Internet' Law Gives Government Sweeping Power Over Internet," NPR, November 1, 2019, https://www.npr.org/2019/11/01/775366588/russian-law-takes-effect-that-gives-government-sweeping-power-over-internet; Adam Satariano and Paul Mozur, "Russia Is Censoring the Internet, With Coercion and Black Boxes," *New York Times*, October 22, 2021, https://www.nytimes.com/2021/10/22/technology/russia-internet-censorship-putin.html; Craig Timberg, Cat Zakrzewski, and Joseph Menn, "A New Iron Curtain Is Descending Across Russia's Internet," *Washington Post*, March 4, 2022, https://www.washingtonpost.com/technology/2022/03/04/russia-ukraine-internet-cogent-cutoff.

19. Jacob Berntsson and Maygane Janin, "Online Regulation of Terrorist and Harmful Content," *Lawfare* (blog), October 14, 2021, https://www.lawfareblog.com/online-regulation-terrorist-and-harmful-content; Janosch Delcker, "Germany's Balancing Act: Fighting Online Hate While Protecting Free Speech," *Politico*, October 1, 2020, https://www.politico.eu/article/germany-hate-speech-internet-netzdg-controversial-legislation; Ashley Westerman, "'Fake News' Law Goes Into Effect in Singapore, Worrying Free Speech Advocates," NPR, October 2, 2019, https://www.npr.org/2019/10/02/766399689/fake-news-law-goes-into-effect-in-singapore-worrying-free-speech-advocates.

20. Marianne Diaz Hernandez, Rafael Nunes, Felicia Anthonio, and Sage Cheng, "#KeepItOn Update: Who Is Shutting Down the Internet in 2021?," Accessnow, June 7, 2021, https://www.accessnow.org/who-is-shutting-down-the-internet-in-2021; Peter Guest, "In the Dark: Seven Years, 60 Countries, 935 Internet Shutdowns: How Authoritarian Regimes Found an Off Switch for Dissent," Rest of the World, April 26, 2022, https://restofworld.org/2022/blackouts.

21. Mehab Qureshi, "Decoding India's Dubious Distinction as World's 'Internet Shutdown Capital,'" *Indian Express*, December 4, 2021, https://indianexpress.com/article/technology/tech-news-technology/india-ranks-highest-in-internet-suspensions-7654773.

22. "Blockchain Technologies Could Boost the Global Economy U.S.$1.76 Trillion by 2030 Through Raising Levels of Tracking, Tracing and Trust," PwC, October 13, 2020, https://www.pwc.com/gx/en/news-room/press-releases/2020/blockchain-boost-global-economy-track-trace-trust.html.

23. Michael Chui, Mark Collins, and Mark Patel, "IoT Value Set to Accelerate Through 2030: Where and How to Capture It," McKinsey & Company, November 9, 2021, https://www.mckinsey.com/business-functions/mckinsey-digital/our-insights/iot-value-set-to-accelerate-through-2030-where-and-how-to-capture-it.

24. Jack Goldsmith, "The Failure of Internet Freedom," Knight Institute at Columbia University, June 13, 2018, https://knightcolumbia.org/content/failure-internet-freedom; Jack Goldsmith and Andrew Keane Woods, "Internet Speech Will Never Go Back to Normal," *The Atlantic*, April 25, 2020, https://www.theatlantic.com/ideas/archive/2020/04/what-covid-revealed-about-internet/610549.

25. Adrian Shahbaz, "Freedom on the Net 2018: The Rise of Digital Authoritarianism," Freedom House, October 2018, https://freedomhouse.org/report/freedom-net/2018/rise-digital-authoritarianism; Jessica Chen Weiss, "Understanding and Rolling Back Digital Authoritarianism," *War on the Rocks*, February 17, 2020, https://warontherocks.com/2020/02/understanding-and-rolling-back-digital-authoritarianism; Prak Chun Thul, "Cambodia Adopts China-style Internet Gateway Amid Opposition Crackdown," Reuters, February 17, 2021, https://www.reuters.com/business/media-telecom/cambodia-adopts-china-style-internet-gateway-amid-opposition-crackdown-2021-02-17/.

26. Adam Segal, "Peering Into the Future of Sino-Russian Cyber Security Cooperation," *War on the Rocks*, August 10, 2020, https://warontherocks.com/2020/08/peering-into-the-future-of-sino-russian-cyber-security-cooperation; Sino-Russian Cybersecurity Agreement art. 3, April 30, 2015, no. 788-p. https://cyber-peace.org/wp-content/uploads/2013/05/RUS-CHN_CyberSecurityAgreement201504_InofficialTranslation.pdf; Luca Belli, "Cybersecurity Convergence in the BRICS Countries," *Directions*, September 17, 2021, https://directionsblog.eu/cybersecurity-convergence-in-the-brics-countries.

27. "A Declaration for the Future of the Internet," April 28, 2022, https://www.whitehouse.gov/wp-content/uploads/2022/04/Declaration-for-the-Future-for-the-Internet_Launch-Event-Signing-Version_FINAL.pdf.

28. Matthew Slaughter and David McCormick, "Data Is Power," *Foreign Affairs*, April 16, 2021, https://www.foreignaffairs.com/articles/united-states/2021-04-16/data-power-new-rules-digital-age.

29. A zettabyte is one sextillion bytes or 10^{21} (1,000,000,000,000,000,000,000).

30. WEF, "Shaping the Future of Digital Economy and New Value Creation," accessed May 18, 2022, https://www.weforum.org/platforms/shaping-the-future-of-digital-economy-and-new-value-creation.

31. Eric Schmidt, Robert Work, et al., *Final Report: The Beginning of the Beginning* (Washington, D.C.: National Security Commission on Artificial Intelligence, 2021), https://www.nscai.gov/2021-final-report/.

32. Amy Zegart, "Intelligence Isn't Just for Government Anymore," *Foreign Affairs*, November 2, 2020, https://www.foreignaffairs.com/articles/united-states/2020-11-02/intelligence-isnt-just-government-anymore.

33. Lizhi Liu, "The Rise of Data Politics: Digital China and the World," *Studies in Comparative International Development* 56, no. 1 (2021): 45–67, doi: 10.1007/s12116-021-09319-8.

34. "Opinion of the Central Committee of the Communist Party of China and the State Council on Building a More Perfect Market-Based Allocation System and Mechanism for Factors of Production," April 9, 2020, http://www.gov.cn/zhengce/2020-04/09/content_5500622.htm; Rogier Creemers, Johanna Costigan, and Graham Webster, "Translation: Xi Jinping's Speech to the Politburo Study Session on the Digital Economy—Oct. 2021," DigiChina, January 28, 2022, https://digichina.stanford.edu/work/translation-xi-jinpings-speech-to-the-politburo-study-session-on-the-digital-economy-oct-2021.

35. Jake Sullivan, "Remarks at the National Security Commission on Artificial Intelligence Global Emerging Technology Summit," White House press release, July 13, 2021, https://www.whitehouse.gov/nsc/briefing-room/2021/07/13/remarks-by-national-security-advisor-jake-sullivan-at-the-national-security-commission-on-artificial-intelligence-global-emerging-technology-summit.

36. Matt Burgess, "Ignore China's New Data Privacy Law at Your Peril," *Wired*, November 5, 2021, https://www.wired.com/story/china-personal-data-law-pipl; Jack Wagner, "China's Cybersecurity Law: What You Need to Know," *The Diplomat*, June 1, 2017, https://thediplomat.com/2017/06/chinas-cybersecurity-law-what-you-need-to-know.

37. Gary Clyde Hufbauer and Megan Hogan, "Digital Agreements: What's Covered, What's Possible," Peterson Institute for International Economics policy brief, October 2021, https://www.piie.com/reader/publications/policy-briefs/digital-agreements-whats-covered-whats-possible.

38. White House, "Readout of President Biden's Participation in the East Asia Summit," October 27, 2021, https://www.whitehouse.gov/briefing-room/statements-releases/2021/10/27/readout-of-president-bidens-participation-in-the-east-asia-summit.

39. Joshua David, "Hackers Take Down the Most Wired Country in Europe," *Wired*, August 21, 2007, https://www.wired.com/2007/08/ff-estonia/; Elisabeth Bumiller and Thom Shanker, "Panetta Warns of Dire Threat of Cyberattack on U.S.," *New York Times*, October 11, 2012, https://www.nytimes.com/2012/10/12/world/panetta-warns-of-dire-threat-of-cyberattack.html.

40. David Sanger, "Obama Ordered Wave of Cyberattacks Against Iran," *New York Times*, June 1, 2012, https://www.nytimes.com/2012/06/01/world/middleeast/obama-ordered-wave-of-cyberattacks-against-iran.html; Thom Shanker and David Sanger, "U.S. Suspects Iran Was Behind a Wave of Cyberattacks," *New York Times*, October 13, 2012, https://www.nytimes.com/2012/10/14/world/middleeast/us-suspects-iranians-were-behind-a-wave-of-cyberattacks.html; Peter Elkind, "Sony Pictures: Inside the Hack of the Century," *Fortune*, June 25, 2016.

41. Neal Pollard, Adam Segal, and Matthew Devost, "Trust War: Dangerous Trends in Cyber Conflict," *War on the Rocks*, January 16, 2018, https://warontherocks.com/2018/01/trust-war-dangerous-trends-cyber-conflict; Jacquelyn Schneider, "A World Without Trust," *Foreign Affairs*, December 14, 2021, https://www.foreignaffairs.com/articles/world/2021-12-14/world-without-trust.

42. Director of National Intelligence, "Assessing Russian Activities and Intentions in Recent US Elections," January 6, 2017, https://www.dni.gov/files/documents/ICA_2017_01.pdf; U.S. Department of Justice, "Report on the Investigation Into Russian Interference in the 2016 Presidential Election," March 2019, https://www.justice.gov/archives/sco/file/1373816/download.

43. Dustin Voltz, "U.S. Spy Agency Warns That Chinese Hackers Target Military, Defense Industry," *Wall Street Journal*, October 20, 2020, https://www.wsj.com/articles/u-s-spy-agency-warns-beijing-s-hackers-aiming-at-u-s-defense-industry-military-11603206459; Brian Naylor, "One Year After OPM Data Breach, What Has the Government Learned?," NPR, June 6, 2016, https://www.npr.org/sections/alltechconsidered/2016/06/06/480968999/one-year-after-opm-data-breach-what-has-the-government-learned; Office of the National Counterintelligence Executive, "Foreign Spies Stealing U.S. Economic Secrets in Cyberspace," October 2011, https://www.dni.gov/files/documents/Newsroom/Reports%20and%20Pubs/20111103_report_fecie.pdf.

44. Kevin Mandia, "FireEye Shares Details of Recent Cyber Attack, Actions to Protect Community," FireEye, December 8, 2020, https://www.fireeye.com/blog/products-and-services/2020/12/fireeye-shares-details-of-recent-cyber-attack-actions-to-protect-community.html; Gordon Corera, "China Accused of Cyber-Attack on Microsoft Exchange Servers," BBC, July 19, 2021, https://www.bbc.com/news/world-asia-china-57889981.

45. Kim Parker, Juliana Menasce Horowitz, and Rachel Minkin, "How the Coronavirus Outbreak Has—and Hasn't—Changed the Way Americans Work," Pew Research Center, December 9, 2020, https://www.pewresearch.org/social-trends/2020/12/09/how-the-coronavirus-outbreak-has-and-hasnt-changed-the-way-americans-work; Dan Patterson, "Cybercrime Is Thriving During the Pandemic, Driven by Surge in Phishing and Ransomware," CBS News, May 19, 2021, https://www.cbsnews.com/news/ransomware-phishing-cybercrime-pandemic.

46. Ransomware Task Force, "Combatting Ransomware," Institute for Security and Technology, last updated September 23, 2021, https://securityandtechnology.org/wp-content/uploads/2021/09/IST-Ransomware-Task-Force-Report.pdf; Ellen Nakashima, "Cyber Command Has Sought to Disrupt the World's Largest Botnet, Hoping to Reduce Its Potential Impact on the Election," *Washington Post*, October 9, 2020, https://www.washingtonpost.com/national-security/cyber-command-trickbot-disrupt/2020/10/09/19587aae-0a32-11eb-a166-dc429b380d10_story.html; Javier Cordoba and Christopher Sherman, "Cyber Attack Causes Chaos in Costa Rica Government Systems," Associated Press, April 22, 2022, https://apnews.com/article/russia-ukraine-technology-business-gangs-costa-rica-9b2fe3c5a1fba7aa7010eade96a086ea.

47. Davis Hake and Vishaal Hariprasad, "Ransomware's Path to Product/Market Fit," *Net Politics* (blog), September 2, 2021, https://www.cfr.org/blog/ransomwares-path-productmarket-fit; Anthony M. Freed, "How Do Initial Access Brokers Enable Ransomware Attacks?" Cybereason, October 5, 2021, https://www.cybereason.com/blog/how-do-initial-access-brokers-enable-ransomware-attacks.

48. Patrick Howell O'Neill, "Wealthy Cybercriminals Are Using Zero-Day Hacks More Than Ever," *Technology Review*, April 21, 2022, https://www.technologyreview.com/2022/04/21/1050747/cybercriminals-zero-day-hacks.

49. WION Web Team, "Russia Responsible for 74% of Ransomware Attacks in World, Hackers Bagged $400mn in Crypto: Report," WION, last updated February 17, 2022, https://www.wionews.com/world/russia-responsible-for-74-of-ransomware-attacks-in-world-hackers-bagged-400mn-in-crypto-report-453867.

50. U.S. Department of the Treasury, "Treasury Takes Robust Actions to Counter Ransomware," news release, September 21, 2021, https://home.treasury.gov/news/press-releases/jy0364; Alexander Osipovich, "Global Regulators Back Tougher Rules to Prevent Criminals From Using Crypto," *Wall Street Journal*, October 28, 2021, https://www.wsj.com/articles/global-regulators-back-tougher-rules-to-prevent-criminals-from-using-crypto-11635413402?reflink=desktopwebshare_permalink; David Uberti, "How the FBI Got the Colonial Pipeline's Ransom Money Back," *Wall Street Journal*, June 11, 2021, https://www.wsj.com/articles/how-the-fbi-got-colonial-pipelines-ransom-money-back-11623403981.

51. AJ Vicens, "Conti Ransomware Group Announces Support of Russia, Threatens Retaliatory Attacks," CyberScoop, February 25, 2022, https://www.cyberscoop.com/conti-ransomware-russia-ukraine-critical-infrastructure; Catalin Cimpanu, "Conti Ransomware Gang Chats Leaked by Pro-Ukraine Member," *The Record*, February 27, 2022, https://therecord.media/conti-ransomware-gang-chats-leaked-by-pro-ukraine-member.

52. C. Todd Lopez, "In Cyber, Differentiating Between State Actors, Criminals Is a Blur," U.S. Department of Defense, May 14, 2021, https://www.defense.gov/News/News-Stories/Article/Article/2618386/in-cyber-differentiating-between-state-actors-criminals-is-a-blur.

53. Kate Conger, "Hackers' Fake Claims of Ukrainian Surrender Aren't Fooling Anyone. So What's Their Goal?," *New York Times*, April 5, 2022, https://www.nytimes.com/2022/04/05/us/politics/ukraine-russia-hackers.html.

54. Margarita Levin Jaitner, "Russian Information Warfare: Lessons From Ukraine," in *Cyber War in Perspective: Russian Aggression against Ukraine*, ed. Kenneth Geers (Tallinn: NATO CCD COE Publications, 2015), https://ccdcoe.org/uploads/2018/10/Ch10_CyberWarinPerspective_Jaitner.pdf, quoted in Eric Rosenbach and Sue Gordon, "America's Cyber Reckoning," *Foreign Affairs*, December 14, 2021, https://www.foreignaffairs.com/articles/united-states/2021-12-14/americas-cyber-reckoning.

55. Quoted in Alyza Sebinius, "Cyber Command's Annual Legal Conference," *Lawfare* (blog), April 18, 2022, https://www.lawfareblog.com/cyber-commands-annual-legal-conference.

56. Rebecca Slayton, "What Is the Cyber Offense-Defense Balance? Conceptions, Causes, and Assessment," *International Security* 41, no. 3 (2017): 72–109, doi: 10.1162/ISEC_a_00267; Brandon Valeriano, "Does the Cyber Offense Have the Advantage?," Cato Institute, December 20, 2021, https://www.cato.org/commentary/does-cyber-offense-have-advantage.

57. Micah Musser and Ashton Garriott, "Machine Learning and Cybersecurity: Hype and Reality," Center for Security and Emerging Technology, June 2021, https://cset.georgetown.edu/publication/machine-learning-and-cybersecurity.

58. Richard A. Clarke and Robert K. Knake, *Cyber War: The Next Threat to National Security and What to Do About It* (New York: HarperCollins, 2013).

59. Michael P. Fischerkeller and Richard Harknett, "Deterrence Is Not a Credible Strategy for Cyberspace," *Orbis* 61, no. 3 (2017): 381–93, doi: 10.1016/j.orbis.2017.05.003.

60. Joseph S. Nye Jr., "Deterrence and Dissuasion in Cyberspace," *International Security* 41, no. 3 (Winter 2016/2017): 44–71, doi: 10.1162/ISEC_a_00266.

61. U.S. Cyberspace Solarium Commission, *A Warning From Tomorrow*.

62. U.S. Cyber Command, "Achieve and Maintain Cyberspace Superiority," Cyber Command, 2018, https://www.cybercom.mil/Portals/56/Documents/USCYBERCOM%20Vision%20April%202018.pdf?ver=2018-06-14-152556-010.

63. Paul M. Nakasone, "A Cyber Force for Persistent Operations," *Joint Force Quarterly* 92, no. 1 (2019): 10–14, https://ndupress.ndu.edu/Media/News/News-Article-View/Article/1736950/a-cyber-force-for-persistent-operations.

64. Ellen Nakashima, "White House Authorizes Offensive Cyber Operations to Deter Foreign Adversaries," *Washington Post*, September 20, 2018, https://www.washingtonpost.com/world/national-security/trump-authorizes-offensive-cyber-operations-to-deter-foreign-adversaries-bolton-says/2018/09/20/b5880578-bd0b-11e8-b7d2-0773aa1e33da_story.html.

65. John S. McCain National Defense Authorization Act for Fiscal Year 2019, Pub. L. No. 115-232, 132 Stat. 1636–2423 (2018), https://www.govinfo.gov/content/pkg/PLAW-115publ232/pdf/PLAW-115publ232.pdf.

66. Zach Dorfman et al., "Exclusive: Secret Trump Order Gives CIA More Powers to Launch Cyberattacks," Yahoo News, July 15, 2020, https://www.yahoo.com/video/secret-trump-order-gives-cia-more-powers-to-launch-cyberattacks-090015219.html.

67. Brad D. Williams, "CYBERCOM Has Conducted 'Hunt-Forward' Ops in 14 Countries, Deputy Says," *Breaking Defense*, November 10, 2021, https://breakingdefense.com/2021/11/cybercoms-no-2-discusses-hunt-forward-space-cybersecurity-china; Martin Matishak, "Cyber Command Sent a 'Hunt Forward' Team to Help Lithuania Harden Its Systems," *The Record*, May 4, 2022, https://therecord.media/cyber-command-sent-a-hunt-forward-team-to-help-lithuania-harden-its-systems.

68. Ellen Nakashima and Dalton Bennet, "A Ransomware Gang Shut Down After Cybercom Hijacked Its Site and It Discovered It Had Been Hacked," *Washington Post*, November 3, 2021, https://www.washingtonpost.com/national-security/cyber-command-revil-ransomware/2021/11/03/528e03e6-3517-11ec-9bc4-86107e7b0ab1_story.html.

69. AJ Vicens, "U.S. Cyber Command Shares New Samples of Suspected Iranian Hacking Software," CyberScoop, January 12, 2022, https://www.cyberscoop.com/u-s-cyber-command-iranian-hacking-malware-virustotal.

70. Mehul Srivastava et al., "The Secret U.S. Mission to Bolster Ukraine's Cyber Defenses Ahead of Russia's Invasion," *Financial Times*, March 9, 2022, https://www.ft.com/content/1fb2f592-4806-42fd-a6d5-735578651471.

71. Julian Barnes, "U.S. Begins First Cyberoperation Against Russia Aimed at Protecting Elections," *New York Times*, October 23, 2018, https://www.nytimes.com/2018/10/23/us/politics/russian-hacking-usa-cyber-command.html; Ellen Nakashima, "U.S. Cyber Command Operation Disrupted Internet Access of Russian Troll Factory on Day of 2018 Midterms," *Washington Post*, February 27, 2019, https://www.washingtonpost.com/world/national-security/us-cyber-command-operation-disrupted-internet-access-of-russian-troll-factory-on-day-of-2018-midterms/2019/02/26/1827fc9e-36d6-11e9-af5b-b51b7ff322e9_story.html.

72. Christopher A. Ford "The Trouble With Cyber Arms Control," *New Atlantis*, no. 29 (Fall 2010): 52–67; Herb Lin, "Arms Control in Cyberspace: Challenges and Opportunities," *World Politics Review*, March 6, 2012.

73. United Nations Office for Disarmament Affairs, "Group of Governmental Experts," United Nations, accessed May 19, 2022, https://www.un.org/disarmament/group-of-governmental-experts.

74. Group of Governmental Experts on Developments in the Field of Information and Telecommunications in the Context of International Security, Report of the Group of Governmental Experts on Developments in the Field of Information and Telecommunications in the Context of International Security, A/70/174 (July 22, 2015), https://undocs.org/A/70/174.

75. United Nations General Assembly, Resolution 70/237, Developments in the Field of Information and Telecommunications in the Context of International Security, A/RES/70/237 (December 23, 2015), https://undocs.org/A/RES/70/237.

76. Group of Governmental Experts on Developments in the Field of Information and Telecommunications in the Context of International Security, Report of the Group of Governmental Experts on Developments in the Field of Information and Telecommunications in the Context of International Security, A/76/135 (July 14, 2021), https://front.un-arm.org/wp-content/uploads/2021/08/A_76_135-2104030E-1.pdf; Josh Gold, "Unexpectedly, All UN Countries Agreed on a Cybersecurity Report. So What?" *Net Politics* (blog), March 18, 2021, https://www.cfr.org/blog/unexpectedly-all-un-countries-agreed-cybersecurity-report-so-what.

77. Department of Justice, Office of Public Affairs, "U.S. Charges Five Chinese Military Hackers for Cyber Espionage Against U.S. Corporations and a Labor Organization for Commercial Advantage," press release no. 14-528, May 19, 2014, https://www.justice.gov/opa/pr/us-charges-five-chinese-military-hackers-cyber-espionage-against-us-corporations-and-labor; Barack Obama and Xi Jinping, "Remarks by President Obama and President Xi Jinping of the People's Republic of China in Joint Press Conference," White House, September 25, 2015, https://obamawhitehouse.archives.gov/the-press-office/2015/09/25/remarks-president-obama-and-president-xi-peoples-republic-china-joint.

78. FireEye, "Red Line Drawn: China Recalculates Its Use of Cyber Espionage," June 2016, https://www.mandiant.com/media/11416/download; Daniel Paltiel, "G20 Communiqué Agrees on Language to Not Conduct Cyber Economic Espionage," Center for Strategic and International Studies, November 16, 2015, https://www.csis.org/blogs/strategic-technologies-blog/g20-communiqu%C3%A9-agrees-language-not-conduct-cyber-economic; "G7 Declaration on Responsible States Behavior in Cyberspace," Group of Seven, April 11, 2017, https://ccdcoe.org/uploads/2018/11/G7-170411-LuccaDeclaration-1.pdf.

79. Department of Justice, Office of Public Affairs, "Two Chinese Hackers Associated With the Ministry of State Security Charged With Global Computer Intrusion Campaigns Targeting Intellectual Property and Confidential Business Information," press release no. 18-1673, December 20, 2018, https://www.justice.gov/opa/pr/two-chinese-hackers-associated-ministry-state-security-charged-global-computer-intrusion; Christopher Bing, Joseph Menn, and Jack Stubbs, "Inside the West's Failed Fight Against China's 'Cloud Hopper' Hackers," Reuters, June 26, 2019, https://www.reuters.com/investigates/special-report/china-cyber-cloudhopper; Lucian Constantin, "'Five Eyes' Countries Attribute APT10 Attacks to Chinese Intelligence Service," *Security Boulevard*, December 21, 2018, https://securityboulevard.com/2018/12/five-eyes-countries-attribute-apt10-attacks-to-chinese-intelligence-service.

80. White House, "Imposing Costs for Harmful Foreign Activities by the Russian Government," April 15, 2021, https://www.whitehouse.gov/briefing-room/statements-releases/2021/04/15/fact-sheet-imposing-costs-for-harmful-foreign-activities-by-the-russian-government; U.S. Department of the Treasury, "Treasury Sanctions Russia With Sweeping New Sanctions Authority," press release, April 15, 2021, https://home.treasury.gov/news/press-releases/jy0127; Kristen Eichensehr, "SolarWinds: Accountability, Attribution, and Advancing the Ball," Just Security, April 16, 2021, https://www.justsecurity.org/75779/solarwinds-accountability-attribution-and-advancing-the-ball.

81. Garret Hinck and Tim Maurer, "Persistent Enforcement: Criminal Charges as a Response to Nation-State Malicious Cyber Activity," *Journal of National Security Law & Policy* 10, no. 525 (2019–2020): 525–61, quoted in William Akoto, "Hackers for Hire: Proxy Warfare in the Cyber Realm," Modern War Institute, January 31, 2022, https://mwi.usma.edu/hackers-for-hire-proxy-warfare-in-the-cyber-realm/.

82. Department of Justice, Office of Public Affairs, "Six Russian GRU Officers Charged in Connection With Worldwide Deployment of Destructive Malware and Other Disruptive Actions in Cyberspace," press release no. 20-1117, October 19, 2020, https://www.justice.gov/opa/pr/six-russian-gru-officers-charged-connection-worldwide-deployment-destructive-malware-and.

83. Exec. Order No. 13694, "Blocking the Property of Certain Persons Engaging in Significant Malicious Cyber-Enabled Activities," 3 C.F.R. 13694 (2015), https://obamawhitehouse.archives.gov/the-press-office/2015/04/01/executive-order-blocking-property-certain-persons-engaging-significant-m.

84. Jason Bartlett and Megan Ophel, "Sanctions by the Numbers: Spotlight on Cyber Sanctions," Center for a New American Security, May 4, 2021, https://www.cnas.org/publications/reports/sanctions-by-the-numbers-cyber.

85. Exec. Order No. 14024, "Blocking Property With Respect to Specified Harmful Foreign Activities of the Government of the Russian Federation," 86 Fed. Reg. 73 (April 19, 2021), https://www.whitehouse.gov/briefing-room/presidential-actions/2021/04/15/executive-order-on-blocking-property-with-respect-to-specified-harmful-foreign-activities-of-the-government-of-the-russian-federation.

86. Trevor Logan, "U.S. Should Indict and Sanction Cyber Adversaries," Foundation for Defense of Democracies, February 27, 2019, https://www.fdd.org/analysis/2019/02/27/u-s-should-indict-and-sanction-cyber-adversaries.

87. Jared Cohen and Richard Fontaine, "Uniting the Techno-Democracies: How to Build Digital Cooperation," *Foreign Affairs*, October 13, 2020, https://www.foreignaffairs.com/articles/united-states/2020-10-13/uniting-techno-democracies; Martijin Rasser, "The Case for an Alliance of Techno-Democracies," Observer Research Foundation, October 19, 2021, https://www.orfonline.org/expert-speak/the-case-for-an-alliance-of-techno-democracies.

88. Shinzo Abe, "Defeatism About Japan Is Now Defeated," speech delivered at WEF, January 23, 2019, https://www.weforum.org/agenda/2019/01/abe-speech-transcript.

89. U.S. Department of Commerce, "Global Cross-Border Privacy Rules Declaration," accessed May 19, 2022, https://www.commerce.gov/global-cross-border-privacy-rules-declaration.

90. Jay Heisler, "Smaller Economies See Big Opportunities in Digital Trade Pact," Voice of America, April 21, 2021, https://www.voanews.com/a/economy-business_smaller-economies-see-big-opportunities-digital-trade-pact/6204836.html.

91. Nigel Cory, "U.S. Options to Engage on Digital Trade and Economic Issues in the Asia-Pacific," Information Technology and Innovation Foundation, February 8, 2022, https://itif.org/publications/2022/02/08/us-options-engage-digital-trade-and-economic-issues-asia-pacific.

92. Joshua P. Meltzer, "Why Schrems II Requires US-EU Agreement on Surveillance and Privacy," Brookings TechStream, December 8, 2020, https://www.brookings.edu/techstream/why-schrems-ii-requires-us-eu-agreement-on-surveillance-and-privacy; Kenneth Propp, "Transatlantic Data Transfers: The Slow Motion Crisis," Council on Foreign Relations, January 13, 2021, https://www.cfr.org/report/transatlantic-data-transfers; Matt Burgess, "Europe's Move Against Google Analytics Is Just the Beginning," *Wired*, January 19, 2022, https://www.wired.com/story/google-analytics-europe-austria-privacy-shield/?bxid=5bea07d724c17c6adf15204d&cndid=31936551.

93. White House, "Fact Sheet: United States and European Commission Announce Trans-Atlantic Data Privacy Framework," March 25, 2022, https://www.whitehouse.gov/briefing-room/statements-releases/2022/03/25/fact-sheet-united-states-and-european-commission-announce-trans-atlantic-data-privacy-framework.

94. Paul Karp, "Australia and US Sign Cloud Act Deal to Help Law Enforcement Agencies Demand Data From Tech Giants," *The Guardian*, December 15, 2021, https://www.theguardian.com/technology/2021/dec/16/australia-and-us-sign-cloud-act-deal-to-help-law-enforcement-agencies-demand-data-from-tech-giants.

95. Stewart Baker, "How Can the U.S. Respond to Schrems II?" *Lawfare* (blog), July 21, 2020, https://www.lawfareblog.com/how-can-us-respond-schrems-ii.

96. Department of Justice, Office of Public Affairs, "U.S. Leads Multi-National Action Against 'Gameover Zeus' Botnet and 'Cryptolocker' Ransomware, Charges Botnet Administrator," press release no. 14-584, June 2, 2014, https://www.justice.gov/opa/pr/us-leads-multi-national-action-against-gameover-zeus-botnet-and-cryptolocker-ransomware; Andy Greenberg, "Cops Disrupt Emotet, the Internet's 'Most Dangerous Malware,'" *Wired*, January 27, 2021, https://www.wired.com/story/emotet-botnet-takedown.

97. U.S. Department of Treasury, "U.S. Department of the Treasury Announces Partnership With Israel to Combat Ransomware," press release, November 14, 2021, https://home.treasury.gov/news/press-releases/jy0479.

98. Jonathan Hillman, *The Digital Silk Road: China's Quest to Wire the World and Win the Future* (New York: HarperCollins, 2021); Council on Foreign Relations, *China's Belt and Road: Implications for the United States* (New York: Council on Foreign Relations, 2021).

99. U.S. Cyberspace Solarium Commission, *A Warning From Tomorrow*.

100. "US, Australia and Japan to Fund Undersea Cable in the Pacific," Reuters, December 11, 2021, https://www.voanews.com/a/us-australia-and-japan-to-fund-undersea-cable-in-the-pacific/6350792.html.

101. Annie Njanja, "Google Confirms $1B Investment Into Africa, Including Subsea Cable for Faster Internet," *TechCrunch*, October 6, 2021, https://techcrunch.com/2021/10/06/google-confirms-1b-investment-into-africa-including-subsea-cable-for-faster-internet.

102. "CISA Director Says the LOG4J Security Flaw Is the 'Most Serious' She's Seen in Her Career," CNBC, December 16, 2021, https://www.cnbc.com/video/2021/12/16/cisa-director-says-the-log4j-security-flaw-is-the-most-serious-shes-seen-in-her-career.html.

103. Derek Johnson, "Chinese APT Leveraged Zero Days—Including Log4j—to Compromise U.S. State Governments," *SC Magazine*, March 8, 2022, https://www.

scmagazine.com/analysis/application-security/chinese-apt-leveraged-zero-days-including-log4j-to-compromise-u-s-state-governments.

104. White House, "Readout of White House Meeting on Software Security," January 13, 2022, https://www.whitehouse.gov/briefing-room/statements-releases/2022/01/13/readout-of-white-house-meeting-on-software-security.

105. Schmidt, Work, et al., *Final Report*.

106. White House, "Readout of AUKUS Joint Steering Group Meetings," December 17, 2021, https://www.whitehouse.gov/briefing-room/statements-releases/2021/12/17/readout-of-aukus-joint-steering-group-meetings.

107. Director of National Intelligence, "Assessing Russian Activities and Intentions in Recent US Elections," January 6, 2017, https://www.dni.gov/files/documents/ICA_2017_01.pdf; Select Comm. on Intelligence, Russian Active Measures Campaigns and Interference in the 2016 U.S. Election, S. Rep. No. 116-XX, vol. 1 (2019), https://www.intelligence.senate.gov/sites/default/files/documents/Report_Volume1.pdf; Department of Homeland Security, "Statement by Secretary Jeh Johnson on the Designation of Election Infrastructure as a Critical Infrastructure Subsector," January 6, 2017, https://www.dhs.gov/news/2017/01/06/statement-secretary-johnson-designation-election-infrastructure-critical.

108. Michael Schmitt and Tim Maurer, "Protecting Financial Data in Cyberspace: Precedent for Further Progress on Cyber Norms?," Just Security, August 24, 2017, https://www.justsecurity.org/44411/protecting-financial-data-cyberspace-precedent-progress-cyber-norms; Tim Maurer, Ariel Levite, and George Perkovich, "Toward a Global Norm Against Manipulating the Integrity of Financial Data," Carnegie White Paper, March 27, 2021, https://carnegieendowment.org/2017/03/27/toward-global-norm-against-manipulating-integrity-of-financial-data-pub-68403.

109. Sarah Kreps and Jacquelyn Schneider, "Escalation Firebreaks in the Cyber, Conventional, and Nuclear Domains: Moving Beyond Effects-Based Logics," *Journal of Cybersecurity 5*, no. 1 (2019); Page O. Stoutland and Samantha Pitts-Kiefer, *Nuclear Weapons in the New Cyber Age: Report of Cyber-Nuclear Weapons Study Group*, Nuclear Threat Initiative, September 2018; James M. Acton, "Cyber Warfare & Inadvertent Escalation," *Daedalus* 149, no. 2 (2020): 133–49.

110. Arms Control Association, "U.S. Nuclear Modernization Programs," last updated January 2022, https://www.armscontrol.org/factsheets/USNuclearModernization; Erin D. Dumbacher and Page O. Stoutland, "U.S. Nuclear Weapons Modernization Security and Policy Implications of Integrating Digital Technology," Nuclear Threat Initiative, November 2020, https://media.nti.org/documents/NTI_Modernization2020_FNL-web.pdf.

111. Kim Zetter, "When Russia Helped the U.S. Nab Cybercriminals," Zero Day, November 30, 2021, https://zetter.substack.com/p/when-russia-helped-the-us-nab-cybercriminals.

112. James M. Acton, "Cyber Warfare & Inadvertent Escalation"; Rebecca K.C. Hersman, Eric Brewer, and Suzanne Claeys, "NC3: Challenges Facing the Future System," Center

for International and Strategic Studies, July 9, 2020, https://www.csis.org/analysis/
nc3-challenges-facing-future-system; George Perkovich and Ariel Levite, "How Cyber
Ops Increase the Risk of Accidental Nuclear War," *DefenseOne*, April 21, 2021, https://
www.defenseone.com/ideas/2021/04/how-cyber-ops-increase-risk-accidental-
nuclear-war/173523.

113. Nicole Perlroth, *This is How They Tell Me the World Ends: The Cyber Weapons Arms Race*
(New York: Bloomsbury, 2021).

114. Ellen Nakashima and Craig Timberg, "NSA Officials Worried About the Day Its Potent
Hacking Tool Would Get Loose. Then It Did," *Washington Post*, May 16, 2017, https://
www.washingtonpost.com/business/technology/nsa-officials-worried-about-the-day-
its-potent-hacking-tool-would-get-loose-then-it-did/2017/05/16/50670b16-3978-
11e7-a058-ddbb23c75d82_story.html.

115. Ari Schwartz and Rob Knake, *Government's Role in Vulnerability Disclosure: Creating a
Permanent and Accountable Vulnerabilities Equities Process* (Cambridge, MA: Belfer
Center, 2016); Michael Daniel, "Heartbleed: Understanding When We Disclose Cyber
Vulnerabilities," *White House Blog*, April 28, 2014, https://www.whitehouse.gov/
blog/2014/04/28/heartbleed-understanding-when-we-disclose-cyber-vulnerabilities.

116. *China's Capabilities for State-Sponsored Cyber Espionage: Testimony Before the U.S.-China
Economic and Security Review Commission*, 117th Cong. (February 17, 2022) (statement
of Kelli Vanderlee, Senior Manager, Strategic Analysis, Mandiant Threat Intelligence),
https://www.uscc.gov/sites/default/files/2022-02/Kelli_Vanderlee_Testimony.pdf; Zeyi
Yang, "Beijing Punishes Alibaba for Not Reporting Log4j Loophole Fast Enough,"
Protocol, December 22, 2021, https://www.protocol.com/bulletins/alibaba-
cloud-log4j#.

117. Lily Hay Newman, "Hackers Are Getting Caught Exploiting New Bugs More Than
Ever," *Wired*, April 21, 2022, https://www.wired.com/story/zero-day-exploits-
vulnerabilities-google-mandiant.

118. Australian Signals Directorate, "Responsible Release Principles for Cyber Security
Vulnerabilities," accessed May 20, 2022, https://www.asd.gov.au/responsible-release-
principles-cyber-security-vulnerabilities; Communication Security Establishment,
"CSE's Equities Management Framework," last updated March 11, 2019, https://cse-
cst.gc.ca/en/information-and-resources/announcements/cses-equities-management-
framework; National Cyber Security Centre, "Equities Process," November 29, 2018,
https://www.ncsc.gov.uk/blog-post/equities-process; Marietje Schaake, *Software
Vulnerability Disclosure in Europe: Technology, Policies, and Legal Challenges* (Brussels:
CEPS, 2018), https://www.ceps.eu/ceps-publications/software-vulnerability-
disclosure-europe-technology-policies-and-legal-challenges.

119. Ellen Nakashima, "Cyber Command Has Sought To Disrupt the World's Largest
Botnet, Hoping To Reduce Its Potential Impact on the Election," *Washington Post*,
October 9, 2020, https://www.washingtonpost.com/national-security/cyber-
command-trickbot-disrupt/2020/10/09/19587aae-0a32-11eb-a166-dc429b380d10_
story.html; Andy Greenberg, "A Trickbot Assault Shows US Military Hackers'
Growing Reach," *Wired*, October 14, 2020, https://www.wired.com/story/
cyber-command-hackers-trickbot-botnet-precedent.

120. Ines Kagubare, "U.S., EU Cyber Investments in Ukraine Pay Off Amid War," *The Hill*, March 13, 2022, https://thehill.com/policy/technology/597921-us-eu-cyber-investments-in-ukraine-pay-off-amid-war.

121. Amy Zegart, "The Weapon the West Used Against Putin," *The Atlantic*, March 5, 2022, https://www.theatlantic.com/ideas/archive/2022/03/russia-ukraine-invasion-classified-intelligence/626557.

122. Michael Schmitt, "Three International Law Rules for Responding Effectively to Cyber Operations," Just Security, July 13, 2021, https://www.justsecurity.org/77402/three-international-law-rules-for-responding-effectively-to-hostile-cyber-operations.

123. Dmitri Alperovitch, "The Case for Cyber Realism," *Foreign Affairs*, December 14, 2021, https://www.foreignaffairs.com/articles/united-states/2021-12-14/case-cyber-realism.

124. Danny Palmer, "The FBI Removed Hacker Backdoors From Vulnerable Microsoft Exchange Servers. Not Everyone Likes the Idea," *ZDNet*, April 19, 2021, https://www.zdnet.com/article/the-fbi-removed-hacker-backdoors-from-vulnerable-microsoft-exchange-servers-not-everyone-likes-the-idea.

125. National Initiative for Cybersecurity Education, "Cybersecurity Workforce Demand," accessed May 20, 2022, https://www.nist.gov/document/workforcedemandone-pager2021finalpdf.

126. White House, "Indo-Pacific Strategy of the United States," February 2022, https://www.whitehouse.gov/wp-content/uploads/2022/02/U.S.-Indo-Pacific-Strategy.pdf.

127. Patrick Howell O'Neill, "Tillerson to Officially Eliminate Cyber Coordinator Office," CyberScoop, August 29, 2017, https://www.cyberscoop.com/state-department-cyber-office-eliminated-rex-tillerson/; State Department, Establishment of the Bureau of Cyberspace and Digital Policy, April 4, 2022, https://www.state.gov/establishment-of-the-bureau-of-cyberspace-and-digital-policy.

128. Suzanne Smalley, "State to Gain More Ability to Monitor DOD Cyber Ops Under White House Agreement," CyberScoop, May 10, 2022, https://www.cyberscoop.com/state-to-gain-authorities-to-monitor-dod-cyber-ops-under-new-white-house-agreement.

129. Kevin Childs and Amy Zegart, "The Divide Between Silicon Valley and Washington Is a National-Security Threat," *The Atlantic*, December 13, 2018, https://www.theatlantic.com/ideas/archive/2018/12/growing-gulf-between-silicon-valley-and-washington/577963.

ACRONYMS

3-D
three dimensional

5G
fifth generation

AI
artificial intelligence

BRI
Belt and Road Initiative

BRICS
Brazil, Russia, India, China, and South Africa

CISA
Cybersecurity and Infrastructure Security Agency

CJEU
The Court of Justice of the European Union

CYBERCOM
U.S. Cyber Command

EU
European Union

GDP
gross domestic product

GDPR
General Data Protection Regulation

GGE
The UN Group of Governmental Experts on Advancing Responsible State Behavior in Cyberspace in the Context of International Security

GRU
Main Intelligence Directorate of Russia

IoT
Internet of Things

ISP
internet service provider

IT
information technology

KORUS
U.S.-Korea Free Trade
Agreement

MSS
Ministry of State Security
of China

NC3
nuclear command, control,
and communications

NATO
North Atlantic Treaty
Organization

NDAA
National Defense
Authorization Act

NSA
National Security Agency

OECD
Organization for Economic
Cooperation and Development

OEWG
Open-Ended Working Group

R&D
research and development

RCEP
The Regional Comprehensive
Economic Partnership

USMCA
U.S.-Mexico-Canada Agreement

VEP
Vulnerabilities Equities Process

VPN
virtual private network

TASK FORCE MEMBERS

Task Force members are asked to join a consensus signifying that they endorse "the general policy thrust and judgments reached by the group, though not necessarily every finding and recommendation." They participate in the Task Force in their individual, not institutional, capacities.

Nicholas F. Beim is a partner at Venrock, a venture capital firm, where he focuses on artificial intelligence, financial technology, and defense investments. His investments include Dataminr, Rebellion Defense, Percipient.ai, Interos, and Altruist. Prior to joining Venrock, Beim was a partner at Matrix Partners and worked in the technology groups at McKinsey & Company and Goldman Sachs. Beim serves on CFR's Board of Directors and on the executive advisory committee of Columbia University's Center on Global Energy Policy. He also serves on the board of directors of Endeavor, a nonprofit organization that supports high-impact entrepreneurs globally.

Elizabeth Bodine-Baron is a senior information scientist at the RAND Corporation specializing in complex networks and systems. She serves as the acting director of the Force Modernization and Employment program in Project AIR FORCE, the only department of the U.S. Air Force's federally funded research and development center concerned entirely with studies and analyses. Her research interests include network analysis and modeling for both domestic and national security issues. Her recent work involves analysis of cyber and information operations, intelligence and targeting tools and processes, and the cybersecurity of logistics and weapon systems. She has used network analysis of social media data to study Russian propaganda, violent extremist messaging, Islamic State support and opposition networks, and information operations. Bodine-Baron received a BS in electrical engineering and a BA in liberal arts from the University of Texas at Austin in 2006, and a PhD in electrical engineering from California Institute of Technology in 2012.

Guillermo S. Christensen is the office managing partner in Washington, DC, for the law firm Ice Miller. Christensen combines his experience as an attorney, a former CIA officer, and a diplomat to inform the advice he provides to clients on cybersecurity and national security law. He has handled numerous cyber incidents but specializes in those involving nation-state or insider threats and ransomware. Christensen's public service includes fifteen years with the CIA in a variety of domestic and international assignments, and from 2010 to 2011 serving as the science and technology advisor to the U.S. Mission to the Organization for Economic Cooperation and Development in Paris. There, Christensen was responsible for advocating for the United States in the technology and telecommunications sectors including cybersecurity, data privacy, cloud computing, and cross-border data flows. Christensen was selected in 2001 by then CIA Director George Tenet to serve as CFR's national intelligence fellow in New York. Christensen currently serves on the international advisory board at William & Mary and is general counsel to the U.S. Association of Cyber Forces.

Michael Dempsey is Northrop Grumman's vice president of strategy and development for space, cyber, and intelligence. He served as acting director of national intelligence in 2017. Between 2014 and 2016, he was deputy director of national intelligence, where he served as President Barack Obama's primary intelligence briefer. He also served as deputy CIA representative to the Joint Chiefs of Staff and director of Western Hemisphere affairs at the National Security Council. He began his intelligence career with the CIA in 1990, serving in a number of positions, including director of the Office of Transnational Issues, director of the Office of Africa, Latin America, and Global Issues, and deputy associate director for military affairs. Prior to that, he served as an artillery officer in the U.S. Army's 101st Airborne Division. Dempsey has received the Presidential Rank Award, two National Intelligence Distinguished Service Awards, the CIA Distinguished Career Intelligence Medal, the Intelligence Community Seal Medallion, the Joint Chiefs of Staff Meritorious Civilian Service Award, and the U.S. Army's Meritorious Service Medal. He earned a BA from Siena College, an MA from Johns Hopkins University's School of Advanced International Studies, and an MA from the University of New York at Albany.

Nathaniel Fick is general manager of Elastic Security, where he leads Elastic's information security business. Previously, he was CEO of the cybersecurity software company Endgame from 2012 through its acquisition by Elastic in 2019. He also led Endgame's professional services business through its acquisition by Accenture in 2017. Fick spent nearly a decade as an operating partner at Bessemer Venture Partners, where he worked with management teams to build durable, high-growth businesses. He spent four years as CEO of the Center for a New American Security in Washington. Fick started his career as a U.S. Marine Corps infantry and reconnaissance officer, including combat tours in Afghanistan and Iraq. His book about that experience, *One Bullet Away*, was a *New York Times* best seller, a *Washington Post* best book of the year, and one of the *Military Times'* best military books of the decade. Fick served two terms as a trustee of Dartmouth College and sits on the military and veterans advisory council at JPMorgan Chase & Co. and on the boards of directors of Strategic Education and Supply Wisdom. He holds a BA in classics from Dartmouth College, an MPA from Harvard Kennedy School, and an MBA from Harvard Business School.

Gordon M. Goldstein is an adjunct senior fellow at CFR. From 2010 to 2018, he was a managing director at Silver Lake, the world's largest investment firm in the global technology industry. Goldstein is a former managing director at Clark & Weinstock and served as a consultant to the Albright Stonebridge Group. He was a senior advisor to the strategic planning unit of the executive office of the UN secretary-general, and codirected the CFR project on the information revolution and the Brookings Institution project on sovereign wealth funds and global public investors. Goldstein is a former Wayland fellow and visiting lecturer at Brown University's Watson Institute for International and Public Affairs. He was a visiting lecturer at the U.S. Defense Intelligence Agency. Goldstein is the author of *Lessons In Disaster: McGeorge Bundy and the Path to War in Vietnam*, which was a *Foreign Affairs* best seller. Goldstein is a graduate of Columbia University, where he was an international fellow and was awarded a BA, MIA, MPhil, and PhD in political science and international relations. He continues his affiliation with the university as a nonresident fellow of Columbia Law School's Roger Hertog Program on Law and National Security. He is a member of the advisory board for the Columbia University School of International and Public Affairs.

Vishaal Hariprasad is the cofounder and CEO of Resilience, a Silicon Valley–based cyber insurance startup. Prior to that, he served as a cyber operations officer for the U.S. Air Force, with multiple combat assignments overseas, and with the National Security Agency. Hariprasad then cofounded Morta Security (acquired by Palo Alto Networks), launched the Cyber Threat Alliance at Palo Alto Networks Unit 42, and became a partner at the Pentagon's Defense Innovation Unit Experimental in Mountain View, California. He is currently a major in the Air Force Reserves and is the Individual Mobilization Augmentee director of operations for the 90th Cyber Operations Squadron in San Antonio, Texas, where he focuses on leading tool development for cyber operations. Hariprasad also received the Bronze Star from the 36th Infantry Division and combat spurs from the 3rd Armored Cavalry for his service in Iraq, making him one of the few official Air Force Cavalrymen. He holds a BA in mathematics from the U.S. Air Force Academy.

Niloofar Razi Howe is a senior operating partner at Energy Impact Partners, a venture capital fund investing in companies shaping the energy landscape of the future. She serves on the boards of directors of Tenable, Composecure, Morgan Stanley Banks, Pondurance (as executive chair), Recorded Future, Swimlane, and Tamr. Howe is a fellow at the International Security Initiative at New America and serves on a number of U.S. government advisory boards. Her nonprofit work includes serving on the board of IREX (as chair) and as a member of the board of trustees of the Smithsonian National Museum of Asian Art. Previously, Howe served as senior vice president of strategy and operations at RSA, a global cybersecurity company, and as the chief strategy officer of Endgame, a leading enterprise software security company. Prior to her operating roles, she spent twelve years leading deal teams in private equity and venture capital at both Paladin Capital Group and Zone Ventures. Howe started her professional career as a lawyer with O'Melveny & Myers and as a consultant with McKinsey & Company. She holds a BA from Columbia College and a JD from Harvard Law School.

Will Hurd is a managing director at Allen & Company. He is growing the U.S. transatlantic partnership with Europe as a trustee of the German Marshall Fund, and, as a member of OpenAI's board of directors, helps build safe artificial general intelligence. Prior to representing his hometown of San Antonio, Texas, in Congress, he was a cybersecurity executive and undercover officer in the CIA. Hurd is the author of *American Reboot: An Idealist Guide to Getting Big Things Done.*

Richard H. Ledgett Jr. has over four decades of intelligence and cyber experience, including twenty-nine years with the National Security Agency, where he served as deputy director from January 2014 until his retirement in April 2017. Ledgett led NSA's Media Leaks task force, NSA's 24/7 Cyber Threat Operations Center, global language and analytic operations, global collection and cryptanalytic operations, and all NSA operations in the Pacific. Ledgett was the Intelligence Community's (IC) first national intelligence manager for cyber, serving as principal advisor to the director of national intelligence (DNI) on all cyber matters. He was also the DNI's director for collection, overseeing all of the IC's collection programs. His civilian awards include the National Security Medal, the Distinguished and Meritorious Presidential Rank Awards, the National Intelligence Distinguished and Superior Service Medals, the Department of Defense Distinguished Civilian Service Award, the Chairman of the Joint Chiefs of Staff Joint Meritorious Civilian Service Award, the NSA Distinguished Civilian Service Medal, the NSA Exceptional and Meritorious Civilian Service Awards, and the CIA Donovan Award. Ledgett is a member of the National Infrastructure Advisory Council and serves on several corporate boards and startup advisory boards.

Shelley B. Leibowitz is a prominent technology advisor, thought leader, and director. She has spent her career at the intersection of financial services and technology, with both private sector and public sector experience. After more than two decades of chief information officer roles at top tier financial services companies, Leibowitz served as group-wide chief information officer for the World Bank. Leibowitz is also a seasoned corporate director and serves on the boards of Elastic NV and Morgan Stanley, as well as several privately held companies in the fintech and information security arena. She also advises companies in areas of digital transformation, information technology portfolio and risk management, information security and digital trust, performance metrics, and effective governance. She serves on the advisory board of the Center for Development Economics at Williams College, the Center for a New American Security council, the New York board of the National Association of Corporate Directors, and the New York board of BuildOn, a not-for-profit that runs service and learning programs in urban high schools across the country.

Eric H. Loeb is executive vice president of global government affairs at Salesforce. Prior to joining Salesforce in 2018, Loeb served as AT&T's international external affairs senior vice president and on the Global Regulatory Counsel for Concert Communications, PLC, and U.S. Regulatory Counsel for British Telecommunications, PLC. Loeb serves as the chair of the policy pillar on Salesforce's racial equality and justice task force, in addition to being the executive sponsor of WINDforce, an employee equality group representing a worldwide Indigenous network of diversity. He is also an advisory board member of the SEED School of Maryland, the United States Council of International Business, and the Asia Society, Northern California Chapter. Loeb graduated from Bowdoin College and Georgetown University Law Center.

Kimberly Marten is a professor of political science at Barnard College, Columbia University, where she specializes in international security and Russia. She is a faculty member of Columbia's Harriman Institute for Russian, Eurasian and East European Studies, and Saltzman Institute for War and Peace Studies. She has written four books, including *Engaging the Enemy: Organization Theory and Soviet Military Innovation*, which received the Marshall Shulman Prize. CFR published her special report, *Reducing Tensions Between Russia and NATO*, in 2017. In addition to her numerous academic journal articles, her policy pieces have appeared in *Foreign Affairs, Huffington Post, New Republic, New York Times, Washington Quarterly, Washington Post's Monkey Cage* blog, *Lawfare*, and *War on the Rocks*, and she was honored to testify before Congress about Russia's Wagner Group private military company in July 2020. She is a frequent media commentator and appeared on *The Daily Show With Jon Stewart*. She earned her BA at Harvard College and PhD at Stanford University. She is a member of the International Institute for Strategic Studies and is a founding member of PONARS-Eurasia.

Evan S. Medeiros is a professor and Penner family chair in Asia studies at Georgetown University's School of Foreign Service. Medeiros previously served for six years on the staff of the National Security Council as director for China, Mongolia, and Taiwan and then as special assistant to the president and senior director for Asia. Prior to joining the White House, he worked for seven years as a senior political scientist at the RAND Corporation. From 2007 to 2008, he also served at the Treasury Department as a policy advisor on China to Secretary Hank Paulson Jr., working on the U.S.-China Strategic Economic Dialogue. Medeiros is a member of the board of directors of the National Committee on U.S.-China Relations and the international advisory board of Cambridge University's Centre for Geopolitics. Medeiros holds a BA in analytic philosophy from Bates College, an MA in China studies from the School of Oriental and African Studies at the University of London, an MPhil in international relations from the University of Cambridge (as a U.S. Fulbright Scholar), and a PhD in international relations from the London School of Economics and Political Science.

Jami Miscik is CEO and vice chairman of Kissinger Associates, Inc., a strategic international consulting firm that assesses and navigates emerging market geopolitical and macroeconomic risks. Prior to joining Kissinger Associates, Miscik served as the global head of sovereign risk at Lehman Brothers. Before entering the private sector, Miscik had a career in intelligence, ultimately serving as the CIA's deputy director for intelligence. In this role, she was responsible for all of the CIA's intelligence analysts, the production of all-source analysis, and determining the content of the President's Daily Brief. She also served as the director for intelligence programs on the National Security Council. Miscik is vice chair of the CFR Board of Directors, chair at the American Ditchley Foundation, and serves on the boards of Morgan Stanley, General Motors, HP Inc., and In-Q-Tel. From 2009 to 2017, she served on the president's intelligence advisory board and was co-chair from 2014 to 2017. She is a recipient of the Director of Central Intelligence's Director's Medal, the Distinguished Intelligence Medal, the Defense Intelligence Agency Director's Medal, and two Intelligence Commendation Medals. Miscik received her BA from Pepperdine University and her MA from the University of Denver's School of International Studies.

Joseph S. Nye Jr. is university distinguished service professor emeritus and former dean of the Harvard Kennedy School of Government. He has served as assistant secretary of defense for international security affairs, chair of the National Intelligence Council, and a deputy undersecretary of state, and won distinguished service awards from all three agencies. His books include *The Future of Power, The Power Game: A Washington Novel,* and *Do Morals Matter?* He is a fellow of the American Academy of Arts and Sciences, the British Academy, and the American Academy of Diplomacy. In a recent survey of international relations scholars, he was ranked as the most influential scholar on American foreign policy, and in 2011, *Foreign Policy* named him one of the top 100 Global Thinkers. In 2014, Japan awarded him the Order of the Rising Sun. He received his BA from Princeton University, won a Rhodes Scholarship to the University of Oxford, and earned a PhD in political science from Harvard University.

Nicole Perlroth spent a decade as the lead cybersecurity and digital espionage and sabotage reporter for the *New York Times.* Her investigations rooted out Russian hacks of nuclear plants, airports, elections, and petrochemical plants; North Korea's cyberattack against movie studios, banks, and hospitals; Iranian attacks on oil companies, banks, and critical infrastructure; and thousands of Chinese cyberattacks against American businesses, including a months-long hack of the *New York Times.* Perlroth is the author of *This Is How They Tell Me The World Ends*, about the global cyber arms race, which earned the 2021 *Financial Times* and McKinsey Business Book of the Year Award, and producer of a forthcoming documentary and television series based on the book. She serves on the advisory board of a number of cybersecurity start-ups as well as Searle Scholars, which offers grants to support independent biomedical research. Perlroth is a graduate of Princeton University and Stanford University and serves as a regular guest lecturer at the Stanford Graduate School of Business.

Neal A. Pollard is a partner in Ernst & Young's cybersecurity practice and an adjunct professor at Columbia University's School of International and Public Affairs and Georgetown University. Prior to joining Ernst & Young, he was global chief information security officer at UBS. Before his experience in industry and consulting, Pollard was an intelligence officer in the U.S. counterterrorism community, serving managerial and operational assignments in the CIA and the National Counterterrorism Center. In 1996, he founded the Terrorism Research Center and served as a board director and general counsel. For over thirty years, Pollard has worked cybersecurity and cyber operations at every level, from technical operations to law, policy, and strategy, and in government, industry, and academia. He was an international affairs fellow at CFR from 2005 to 2006. He received a BS in mathematics from the University of Oklahoma, an MLitt in international security studies from the University of St Andrews, Scotland, and a JD from the Georgetown University Law Center.

Samantha F. Ravich is the chair of the Center for Cyber and Technology Innovation, a groundbreaking think tank in Washington, DC. She currently sits on the board of directors of International Game Technology, where she is on the NomGov and Compensation Committees and the board of governors of the Gemological Institute of America, where she is on the Audit and R&D Committees. Ravich serves or has served on numerous U.S. government boards and advisory commissions, including the U.S. Secret Service cyber investigations advisory board, the Congressional Cyberspace Solarium Commission, the U.S. secretary of energy's advisory board, the president's intelligence advisory board (where she was co-chair), and the director's advisory board for the National Counterterrorism Center. Ravich worked for Vice President Dick Cheney from 2001 to 2003 when she was an advisor on Asia, the Middle East, and counterterrorism, and was part of the White House staff during 9/11. She was recruited to return from 2005 to 2008, where she served as the vice president's principal deputy national security advisor.

Ted Schlein is a general partner at Kleiner Perkins and executive chairman and founding partner at Ballistic Ventures. Schlein has spent thirty-five years helping to create transformative companies and has served on over fifty public and private company boards. As a company leader, he was the founding CEO of Fortify Software, which was later acquired by Hewlett-Packard. Prior to Kleiner and Ballistic, Schlein served as vice president, enterprise solutions at Symantec. There he led the company's earliest antivirus effort, which included a move into the software utilities market with the launch of a commercial antivirus solution that became the industry gold standard. Schlein is the former chairman of the National Venture Capital Association (NVCA), a national alliance advocating the role of venture investing in job creation, technology innovation, and economic development, and the founder of the Department of Defense–sponsored DeVenCI program. He is an active member of the Cybersecurity and Infrastructure Security Agency's cybersecurity advisory committee, the Homeland Security advisory council, the NSA advisory committee, and the National Security Institute advisory board. Schlein serves on the board of trustees at InQTel, the board of trustees of the University of Pennsylvania, and the dean of advisors of the Engineering School at the University of Pennsylvania. Schlein holds a BA in economics from the University of Pennsylvania.

Adam Segal is the Ira A. Lipman chair in emerging technologies and national security and director of the Digital and Cyberspace Policy program at CFR. Previously, Segal was an arms control analyst for the China Project at the Union of Concerned Scientists. He has been a visiting scholar at Stanford University's Hoover Institution, the Massachusetts Institute of Technology's Center for International Studies, the Shanghai Academy of Social Sciences, and Tsinghua University in Beijing. He has taught at Vassar College and Columbia University. He is the author of *The Hacked World Order: How Nations Fight, Trade, Maneuver, and Manipulate in the Digital Age*, which describes the increasingly contentious geopolitics of cyberspace, *Advantage: How American Innovation Can Overcome the Asian Challenge,* and *Digital Dragon: High-Technology Enterprises in China.* His work has appeared in the *Economist, Financial Times, Foreign Affairs, Foreign Policy,* and *Wall Street Journal,* among others, and he has written articles and book chapters on Chinese technology policy. Segal has a BA and PhD in government from Cornell University and an MA in international relations from Tufts University's Fletcher School of Law and Diplomacy.

Camille A. Stewart is the global head of product security strategy at Google, where she leads federated security for the company. Previously, Stewart led security, privacy, election integrity, and dis/misinformation efforts for Google's mobile business as the head of security policy for Google Play and Android. Prior to Google, she managed cybersecurity, election security, tech innovation, and risk issues at Deloitte. She was appointed by President Obama as the senior policy advisor for cyber infrastructure and resilience policy at the Department of Homeland Security. She was the senior manager of legal affairs at Cyveillance, a cybersecurity company, after working on Capitol Hill. She also serves on the boards of directors for the International Foundation for Electoral Systems and GirlSecurity and is a member of the Charles F. Bolden Group. Stewart's professional achievements have earned her recognition from a multitude of entities throughout her career, including her selection as 2021 Microsoft Security Changemaker of the Year, 2020 and 2021 cyber fellow at the Harvard Kennedy School's Belfer Center for Science and International Affairs, and the 2019 Cyber Security Women of the Year in the "Barrier Breaker" category.

Philip J. Venables is a vice president at Google and chief information security officer of Google Cloud, where he oversees the risk, security, compliance, and privacy teams. In 2021 he was appointed to President Joe Biden's Council of Advisors on Science and Technology. Previously, he was a partner at Goldman Sachs and during his twenty years there held multiple roles, from chief information security officer and head of technology risk, chief risk officer for operational risk, and private equity operating partner to board director of Goldman Sachs Bank. Earlier in his career, Venables held multiple engineering and security roles for a number of finance, energy, and defense organizations in multiple geographies.

Zaid A. Zaid is the head of U.S. public policy at Cloudflare and was previously the head of North America for strategic response policy at Meta. Zaid served on the Biden/Harris transition on the Agency Review Teams for the U.S. Department of State and the International Development Agencies. He was special assistant to President Obama and associate White House counsel and senior attorney advisor to the general counsel at the U.S. Agency for International Development (USAID). He joined the Obama administration from WilmerHale. Prior to law school, he was a political officer in the Foreign Service. He served in Baghdad, Cairo, Tunis, and the U.S. Mission to the United Nations. Zaid holds degrees from Columbia Law School, the Fletcher School, and Georgetown University. Zaid is a senior fellow at the Center for the Study of the Presidency and Congress and a Truman National Security Project fellow. He serves on the advisory committee at the Council of Global Equality, the board of iMMAP, the board of governors at Georgetown University, and the board of advisors of the Walsh School of Foreign Service.

Amy B. Zegart is the Morris Arnold and Nona Jean Cox senior fellow at the Hoover Institution and professor of political science by courtesy at Stanford University. She is also the founding codirector of Stanford University's cyber policy program and a contributing writer at the *Atlantic*. She specializes in U.S. intelligence, emerging technologies and national security, and global political risk management. Zegart is the award-winning author of five books, including *Spies, Lies, and Algorithms: The History and Future of American Intelligence* (2022); *Bytes, Bombs, and Spies: The Strategic Dimensions of Offensive Cyber Operations* (2019), coedited with Herbert Lin; and *Political Risk: How Businesses and Organizations Can Anticipate Global Insecurity* (2018), coauthored with Condoleezza Rice. Zegart's op-eds and essays have appeared in *Foreign Affairs, Politico, New York Times, Washington Post, Wall Street Journal, Wired*, and elsewhere. Previously, she spent four years as a McKinsey & Company consultant, served on the Clinton administration's National Security Council staff, and was a foreign policy adviser to the Bush 2000 presidential campaign. She received an AB in East Asian studies from Harvard College and an MA and PhD in political science from Stanford University.

TASK FORCE OBSERVERS

Observers participate in Task Force discussions but are not asked to join the consensus. They participate in their individual, not institutional, capacities.

Thomas E. Graham is a distinguished fellow at CFR, a lecturer in global affairs and political science at Yale University, and a research fellow at the MacMillan Center at Yale. He is a cofounder of the Russian, East European, and Eurasian studies program at Yale University and sits on its faculty steering committee. Previously, Graham was special assistant to the president and senior director for Russia on the National Security Council (NSC) staff from 2004 to 2007 and NSC director for Russian affairs from 2002 to 2004. He was a Foreign Service officer for fourteen years, with assignments at the U.S. Embassy in Moscow in the late Soviet period and the mid-1990s, during which he served as head of the political internal unit and acting political counselor. Between tours in Moscow, he worked on Russian and Soviet affairs on the policy planning staff at the U.S. Department of State and as a policy assistant in the office of the undersecretary of defense for policy. Graham holds a BA in Russian studies from Yale University and an MA in history and a PhD in political science from Harvard University.

Lauren Kahn is a research fellow at CFR, where her work focuses on defense innovation and the impact of emerging technologies on international security, with a particular emphasis on artificial intelligence. Prior to joining CFR, Kahn worked as a research fellow at Perry World House, the University of Pennsylvania's global policy think tank, where she helped launch and run its project on emerging technologies and global politics. Her work has appeared in *Bulletin of the Atomic Scientists*, Defense One, *Foreign Affairs, Lawfare, Orbis*, and

War on the Rocks, and has been featured in the *Economist.* She received her bachelor's degree in international relations from the University of Pennsylvania and is currently pursuing a master's degree in computer and information technology at the University of Pennsylvania's School of Engineering and Applied Sciences.

Rafi Martina serves as senior advisor to the chairman of the Senate Select Committee on Intelligence. Prior to joining the committee staff, he served as senior technology counsel for Senator Mark Warner (D-VA), acting as the senator's principal advisor on technology, telecommunications, consumer protection, and trade issues. He oversaw Senator Warner's pioneering work on platform regulation, leading the drafting of the senator's influential 2018 white paper on addressing disinformation, market concentration, and consumer harms posed by large technology platforms. Prior to joining Senator Warner's staff, Martina served as regulatory counsel for Sprint from 2011 to 2015, where he represented Sprint in major rulemaking proceedings, mergers and acquisitions, and cases before the Federal Communications Commission (FCC), the National Telecommunications and Information Administration, the Department of Justice, and federal courts. Before joining Sprint, Martina was the recipient of a postgraduate fellowship from the University of Virginia School of Law Foundation, through which he acted as a legal fellow and staff attorney for FCC Commissioner Meredith Attwell Baker from 2010 to 2011. Martina received his BA in political science and science, technology, and society from the University of Michigan and was a visiting scholar at the University of Oxford's Worcester College. He graduated from the University of Virginia School of Law.

Shannon K. O'Neil is the vice president, deputy director of studies, and Nelson and David Rockefeller senior fellow for Latin America Studies at CFR. She is an expert on Latin America, global trade, U.S.-Mexico relations, corruption, democracy, and immigration. O'Neil is the author of the forthcoming *The Globalization Myth: Why Regions Matter,* which chronicles the rise of three main global manufacturing and supply chain hubs and what they mean for U.S. economic competitiveness. She also wrote *Two Nations Indivisible: Mexico, the United States, and the Road Ahead,* which analyzes the political, economic, and social transformations Mexico has undergone over the last three decades and why they matter for the United States. She is a columnist for Bloomberg Opinion and a frequent guest on national broadcast news and radio programs. O'Neil has often testified before Congress and regularly speaks at global academic, business, and policy conferences. O'Neil has lived and worked in Argentina and Mexico. She was a Fulbright Scholar and a Justice, Welfare, and Economics fellow at Harvard University, and has taught Latin American politics at Columbia University. Before turning to policy, O'Neil worked in the private sector as an equity analyst at Indosuez Capital and Credit Lyonnais Securities. She holds a BA from Yale University, an MA in international relations from Yale University, and a PhD in government from Harvard University. She is a member of the board of directors of the Tinker Foundation.

Stewart M. Patrick is the James H. Binger senior fellow in global governance and the director of the International Institutions and Global Governance program at CFR. From 2005 to 2008, he was a research fellow at the Center for Global Development, where he directed research and policymaking at the intersection of security and development. Patrick has also served on the U.S. State Department's policy planning staff, where he was responsible for U.S. policy toward Afghanistan and a range of global and transnational issues. Prior to government service, he was a research associate at New York University's Center on International Cooperation. He has taught at Johns Hopkins University's School of Advanced International Studies and at New York University. The author of *The Sovereignty Wars: Reconciling America With the World*, Patrick has also written, cowritten, or edited five books, including *Weak Links: Fragile States, Global Threats, and International Security*. He also writes the *Internationalist* blog for CFR. Patrick received a bachelor's degree from Stanford University and two master's degrees and a doctorate in international relations from the University of Oxford, where he was a Rhodes Scholar.

James A. Ryans II, of the U.S. Marine Corps, most recently served as senior military assistant to the Secretary of the Navy and as the deputy commander of Taskforce Southwest, a task-organized Marine unit designed to deploy to Afghanistan. Colonel Ryans previously served as commanding officer of the Eighth Marine Regiment, Second Marine Division, in Camp Lejeune, North Carolina. He has also served in the Second Marine Division as a rifle platoon commander and rifle company executive officer in the First Battalion Eighth Marines, a rifle company commander in the Second Battalion Eighth Marines, and a battalion commander in the Third Battalion Sixth Marines, and as the commanding officer of Headquarters Battalion. Colonel Ryans served as assistant operations officer, operations officer, and executive officer of the Eighth Marine Regiment. Additionally, he has served as the future operations officer of the II Marine Expeditionary Force, with Marine Corps Recruiting command, with Marine Aviation Weapons and Tactics Squadron 1, and the Joint Staff. He has completed multiple combat deployments and participated in Operation Silver Wake, Operation Iraqi Freedom, and Operation Enduring Freedom. Colonel Ryans graduated from Jacksonville University with a BS in physics and completed the advanced management program at Harvard Business School in 2018. He also attended the following military schools: Infantry Captains Career Course, Marine Corps Command and Staff College, and the Naval War College.

Anya Schmemann (ex officio) is Washington director of global communications and outreach and director of the Independent Task Force Program at CFR in Washington, DC. Schmemann has overseen numerous high-level Task Forces on a wide range of topics, including China's Belt and Road Initiative, pandemic preparedness, innovation, the future of work, Arctic strategy, nuclear weapons, climate change, immigration, trade policy, and internet governance, as well as on U.S. policy toward Afghanistan, Brazil, North Korea, Pakistan, and Turkey. She previously served as assistant dean for communications and outreach at American University's School of International Service and managed communications at Harvard Kennedy School's Belfer Center for Science and International Affairs, where she also administered the Caspian studies program. She coordinated a research project on Russian security issues at the EastWest Institute in New York and was assistant director of CFR's Center for Preventive Action in New York, focusing on the Balkans and Central Asia. She was a Truman National Security Project fellow and is co-chair of the Global Kids DC advisory council. Schmemann received a BA in government and an MA in Russian studies from Harvard University.

Matthew C. Waxman is adjunct senior fellow for law and foreign policy at CFR. He is also the Liviu Librescu professor of law at Columbia Law School, and he previously served as co-chair of the Cybersecurity Center at Columbia University's Data Science Institute. Before joining the Columbia faculty, he served at the U.S. Department of State as principal deputy director of policy planning. His prior government appointments include deputy assistant secretary of defense for detainee affairs, director for contingency planning and international justice at the National Security Council, and executive assistant to the national security adviser. After law school he served as law clerk to Supreme Court Justice David H. Souter and U.S. Court of Appeals Judge Joel M. Flaum. His publications include *The Dynamics of Coercion: American Foreign Policy and the Limits of Military Might* and a forthcoming edited volume, *The Future Law of Armed Conflict*. Waxman is a graduate of Yale College and Yale Law School and studied international relations as a Fulbright Scholar in the United Kingdom.

Contributing CFR Staff

Marcelo Agudo
Senior Editor, Publications

Dalia Albarrán
Senior Graphic Designer,
Digital Services

Maria Teresa Alzuru
Deputy Director of Product
Management, Digital Services

Sabine Baumgartner
Senior Photo Editor,
Digital Services

Michael Bricknell
Data Visualization Designer,
Digital Services

Patricia Lee Dorff
Editorial Director, Publications

Kyle Fendorf
Research Associate, Digital
and Cyberspace Policy

Will Merrow
Associate Director of Data
Visualization, Digital Services

Anya Schmemann
Director, Independent Task
Force Program

Chelie Setzer
Associate Director, Independent
Task Force Program

Connor Sutherland
Program Coordinator, Washington
Meetings and Independent Task
Force Program

Contributing Interns

Caroline Allen
Independent Task Force Program

Kevin Bloodworth
Independent Task Force Program

Jaleah Cullors
Independent Task Force Program

Anika Mirza
Independent Task Force Program